T0194161

Chick Flicks Lie

Sugar-free Accounts of a Positive Pessimist

HOLLY MARIE TONG

authorHOUSE®

AuthorHouse™ LLC
1663 Liberty Drive
Bloomington, IN 47403
www.authorhouse.com
Phone: 1-800-839-8640

Cover photography by Shannon Fontaine
www.shannonfontaine.com

Published by AuthorHouse 4/14/2014

ISBN: 978-1-4918-9866-6 (sc)
ISBN: 978-1-4918-9864-2 (hc)
ISBN: 978-1-4918-9865-9 (e)

CONTENTS

ACKNOWLEDGEMENTS

First and foremost, I want to thank our Lord and Savior Jesus Christ for his love, forgiveness, strength, and resources which made this project possible. He knows just how imperfect I really am, and he knows dating hasn't exactly been my strong suit, yet he loves me anyways. I haven't always been obedient, and I haven't always listened. I haven't always dated the good boys, and I haven't always been careful with other people's hearts, yet he still chooses to work on me and bless me. I thank him for laughter, and for the strength he has given me to learn from my experiences. Life between dating and marriage may not always be a walk in the park, but he is faithful, and I always know he alone offers more than anything in this world ever could. He is my ultimate source of happiness, and I wholeheartedly believe in his perfect timing.

Next up, my dear family – I cannot thank you guys enough for EVERYTHING. Thank you for always being there and thank you for always believing in me. We all know the Nashville journey hasn't been an easy one for me, but I do know it is God and you who keep me going here.

Dad – You've always been the rock of our family and the strongest man I know (literally and metaphorically). From you, I inherited a love for being creative, an abnormally strong work ethic and "dreamer blood." I may not have a husband just yet, but I do have the world's best Dad, who reminds me good, faithful men still exist. I truly believe God knew I was going to need a Dad like you to keep my belief in love alive and to help me through life…so he just happened to send me the best example possible. We've come a long way on this dream journey, and we're just getting started. Thank you for everything you are. Love, your baby girl.

Mom – I could write a whole book just on the conversations you've had to endure with me over the years. Words cannot express my thanks to you for your love, your understanding, and your patience. At the end of the day, you are the person who is ALWAYS willing to listen to me no matter how repetitive or exhausting I may be. I'm still convinced you are a super hero without a cape. You are talented, admirably domesticated, and beautiful inside and out. Your contagious laugh is one of my favorite sounds in the world.

Brother Aaron & Sister-In-Law Nicole – Thanks for being another example of good, faithful love. I'll never settle for anything less than what you two, and Mom and Dad have. Nieces Christina and Caylin.. and nephew Carson – You guys are my joy. I may not be a mother yet, but since I have such sweet nieces and an amazing nephew, being an Aunt is just fine for now!

Austin – You are yet another example of a real man. Sometimes I think you're the male version of me, and that I'm the female version of you….so with that said, go for those dreams of yours…I believe in you.

Haley – My amazing little sis…from the day you were born, we not only had a sisterly bond, but also a mother/daughter-like kind of bond. I think somehow God knew I needed an over a decade younger sister. Thanks for keeping me sane and keeping me young. You are the sunshine of my life. Just please don't tie the knot before me (like the upcoming "Leah scenario" in this book), k?

Grandma Tong – I admired your poetry growing up. You were a great writing influence. I'm glad I got to share some of my journey with you…even though it wasn't nearly long enough. Somehow as I write this, I can still hear your sweet subtle chuckle, and imagine you'd get a kick out of this whole book-writing ordeal. Thank you for being one of the best Godly examples I'll ever know.

Special thanks to my true blue friends, and of course my second family away from home. All of you know exactly who you are. I couldn't have survived this crazy ride without you. Thanks for the talks, the laughs, the encouragement, and the prayers.

Huge thanks to everyone in Music City who has believed in me, guided me, and taken me under their wing. Your faces are running through my mind as I write this. I wish I could list all of you individually, but since the list is so long, I'm terrified I'd forget someone. If I were to really list everyone and their lasting impact…it would undoubtedly be a whole book in itself. You're all so special in so many ways. Nashville could have been a culture shock for this small town gal when I moved here nine years ago, but instead it felt and feels like a family community. It feels like home, and I have all of you to thank for that.

Sonya Thompson – Behind every good writer is a great editor. Thank you for believing in me, and thank you for taking on this massive project. You are a true blessing, and I appreciate you more than you'll ever know.

Shannon Fontaine – You are an incredible photographer, and you couldn't have done a better job of "capturing" the needed image. I needed someone to "complete" this project. You met and exceeded any and all expectations I had.

Harlow Salon on Music Row– Shana Dyer, thank you for always making me as pretty of a positive pessimist as possible. Though I haven't made it to the altar yet, all the guys in my life thus far have loved my hair, thanks to you. You're a true rock star! To the entire Harlow staff, thank you so much for holding my book signing party. I have faith that it's going to be a success, and I cannot express my gratitude enough.

Last, but certainly not least, thank you to my Kindergarten teacher Mrs. Gassman who taught me how to properly hold a pencil. Quite obviously, this simple detail has been undoubtedly vital as a writer.

PREFACE

First of all, this is not a "how-to" book, friends…because let's face it, if I knew how, I wouldn't be writing it. I would instead be oozing in the awesomeness of my Mr. Wonderful while I play Betty Crocker in my massive kitchen of perfection. I am not going to sugarcoat anything. This is a sugar-free book, because I am a sugar-free girl. (Well, except for the sugar-filled treats that I have to indulge in following a breakup). This book isn't about structure, because most dating lives are anything but structural. They are instead jumbled up, unruly, all over the place, and completely out of control. Thus this book will match this modern disorganization.

This project is just a laughable account of some of the trials, tribulations, and downright hilarious moments that can happen in a typical dating life…or a not so typical dating life. Additionally, this is a light-hearted look at Hollywood's commercially exaggerated messages which are so often present in our beloved chick flicks. As I have figured out, and I'm sure that many of you have: Chick flicks are sweet, but they are pathological liars. As the title of this book implies, I have A LOT to say about the irresistible silver screen bunk (which I just happen to immerse myself in, despite the deception)…so please read on.

Before we get into all of the above though, it is important to address what is intended by the term "positive pessimist" in this particular book. In my definition, a positive pessimist within the dating realm is not negative about life in general. In fact, they are quite positive, despite the adversities that often come their way. A positive pessimist knows how to laugh at themselves and at their failed relationships. They often find a way to laugh rather than cry right then and there in the face of heartbreak. They are polite and entertaining to be around even when they're enduring trials. Positive pessimists do not deny what is in their rearview mirror. Consequently, they own their stories, and they're not ashamed of their unsuccessful dating track record. In fact, they find their messes to be downright hilarious at times.

Not only are these positive pessimists I speak of full of laughter, they are also wise, experienced, and seasoned in the dating department. These individuals may remain cynical or skeptical about the prospects around them, but it's because they have learned a thing or two. They have learned from their past experiences both good and bad, and they tuck their wisdom in the back of their minds. They know what to look for and what not to look for in the opposite sex. They don't ignore hunches, red flags, or caution signs. They take what their gut has to say very seriously, and they weigh out the possibilities without letting their emotions trump common sense. A positive pessimist is not easily blindsided or naively fooled by a man's smooth talking sales-like pitch. They look both ways before crossing the line, and they test the waters before jumping in. A person of this character recognizes their own flaws, and remains positive about life and the lessons they've learned. As a result, they have great hope for the future. They prove that owning a tough story doesn't have to make a person negative. Deep down, they believe everything will be okay one way or another…single or taken.

They don't necessarily go out on a first date expecting the person picking them up to be their one, but they do go in open to the possibility. If their date goes horribly wrong, they have yet another story to laugh about with their best friends. They know that life is about experiencing everything put in their paths, and it is what they make of it. Not all of it is good, but they remain alert, and positive in the midst of their skepticism. If things go wrong…the positive pessimist just laughs it off, and writes a book to cheer everyone up in the process.

With that said, one day I found myself stewing over my own chaotic dating life and thought, "I could write a book." Then I thought, "Hey, maybe I will!" That day happened around five years ago, but I cannot say the exact time for sure. My memory is fading as the years go by. That's what happens when you're in the expedited process of turning into an old maid. As a seasoned 29 year old who is currently flirting with 30, I have experienced a little bit of everything. So here we are, folks.

In case you are wondering, some of the accounts you are about to read did indeed happen to me. However, this book is far from a confessional of my life, or a "bash on all my exes" project (though I did find a way to inconspicuously slam several of them). I repeat though: This is NOT a "Holly Marie Tong confessional." Several scenarios you come across may have happened to someone I know, while others entered my head because they sounded appropriate for today's messy dating world. I let my imagination run wild during this project. If I were to tell you which accounts are which, it wouldn't be nearly as fun. Therefore, I have tweaked, plucked, altered, and modified my own personal stories to the point where they are as unrecognizable as a movie star after a failed Botox injection. My intention is not for anyone to get bent out of shape over anything. This light-hearted read is just simply designed to be an entertaining compilation of crazy situations which I believe many of you will find relatable. If not, I hope you will at least get a good laugh out of today's dating dysfunctions.

I don't know where you are in your dating, seeing, hanging out, talking, official, non-Facebook official, engaged, married, or single as cheese without macaroni life, but I believe this book will put a smile on your face, especially if you are in the place that I am in as I write this. Sometimes it is good to know that you're not alone, that someone shares in your understanding, your disappointments, your soap opera drama, and your own personal reality show…which you never planned to star in. For me personally, faith and laughter have been the best medicines on this confusing, frustrating, crazy, deranged, yet sometimes downright funny journey. If you haven't yet discovered the importance of faith and laughter during love's trials, I hope this book opens you up to the priceless concept which has become an everyday necessity for me.

If you've experienced one heart-wrenching breakup in your life, this book is for you. If someone you love has gone through relationship troubles, this book is for you. If you're good at finding bad boys and bad at finding good boys, this book is for you. If you've given up a perfectly suitable guy "just because," this book is for you. If you hear, "I've never seen this happen before" on a weekly basis, this book is for you. If you just want to laugh it up, and go on a journey of positive pessimism, this book is for you. If you're only reading this to find out if you're in it, or simply because you love me or hate me…this book is for you. Rest assured if "you" are in it, I have changed your name. Though I greatly admire and appreciate Taylor Swift's calling out of her exes, in my case, I would rather ensure that several of mine don't even get the satisfaction of having their names appear in print. However, if you are in here, thank you in advance for being my inspiration. You are the frosting to my cake…which may or may not be sugar-filled.

INTRODUCTION

I remember the first time I watched the famous Disney classic that we all know as Cinderella. I felt like I was in her shoes…or should I say glass slippers? I felt like I had to slave my life away and just watch my dreams pass me by. That is, until the fairy godmother came along and "voila," she went from rags to riches in the blink of an eye. She caught Prince Charming's beautiful eye, and they lived happily ever after. Cinderella got her rainbow, but not after first experiencing the rain. She suffered, but she persevered…beautifully.

Likewise, I remember the first time I watched "The Wizard of Oz." I was completely, helplessly, and utterly intrigued from the get-go. I identified with Dorothy Gale because she was just a down home farm girl always looking beyond that fencerow, and dreaming of somewhere over the rainbow. Like Dorothy, I was the little farm girl with pigtails who talked entirely too fast and too much for those who lived with me to keep up. The Kansas girl in the plaid dress didn't particularly have a love interest, but she dreamed just like a child. She loved her family and her home, but she experienced a restlessness which couldn't be denied. Maybe it was the ruby red slippers, the vibrant colors, my fascination with shiny objects, or the adorable "Toto," but this movie was one that would be watched time and time again. Like Dorothy, I was always dreaming of something more and trying to run away. However, at the end of the day I always found it was the people in my life who would always surpass any dream that I dared to dream.

Then I turned sixteen and "chick flicks" became my ultimate cup of tea. Why? Probably because boys no longer had cooties, and I was beginning to think that just maybe they could possibly be worth my time and energy. My issues all started at the ball with good ole' Cinderella, then I went on a short girl trip to Emerald City with Dorothy, but it all ultimately came full circle, and I ended up back at the ball on "A Cinderella Story." Yes, if it weren't bad enough that we already had a cartoon about a down on her luck girl being transported in a gigantic pumpkin to Mr. Perfect, we had to go and make an adult version of the highly exaggerated, yet irresistible phenomenon. Dear sweet Cinderella certainly shouldn't take all of the heat though. Noah Calhoun and Allie Hamilton's out of this world Notebook romance didn't help my condition, nor did the countless other tearjerkers I fell in love with. While in the real world I wasn't finding any man who mirrored the Prince Charmings in any of the movies I watched, I always did however, find an uncomfortable resemblance with my choices and the Mr. Wrongs of each movie.

Admittedly, I fell in love with "projects" at an early age, and it just kind of "stuck." As a result of my love for men who needed fixing and magical transformation, I began to kiss frog after frog. Blame it on Hollywood for causing me and countless other gals to believe there could actually be such a thing as "happily ever after." Oftentimes in these painfully unrealistic movies, Prince Charming was flawless from the get-go. In the films where he wasn't initially the quintessential man, he at least became that man by the end. Oh yes, and the famous white horse would always come around to sweep the lady up off her tired feet, and together, they would ride off into the sunset.

Yeah, so I guess you could say Hollywood caused me to form misconceptions and unrealistic dreams. Okay, so I don't just guess they did…I know they did. I found myself dwelling on these fantasies, and had everything but the sappy background music to go along with them. I believed in the quick-fixes of bad boys, the far-fetched scenarios, and the dream-like endings. However, maybe these misconceptions aren't always such a bad thing. Maybe it's okay to temporarily escape reality, and just maybe, you might even end up being the lucky recipient of your own Hollywood fairy tale one day. After all, dreams do come true. Walt

Disney did say, "If you can dream it...you can do it." (SEE, how hard it is to get away from quoting movies and their creators?)

Alright, so, let's fast forward here. One day I woke up and realized I was in high school. That was the day I realized my precious chick flicks were lying to me...and that was the day I began to identify with the Leah Gardowskis of the world. You may be wondering: Who is Leah Gardowski? Leah is a fictional character I created, but she is somewhat me and she is somewhat you. It just so happens she has dated for more than half of her life – yet, she's still a good girl. She isn't the easy, one-night stand type of woman who "needs" a man, but like most of us, she still hopes to end up with a good one in the end. She has probably had more relationships than any of us (though that could be debatable), but she is the representation of a woman who has seen it all. She is the classic down-to-earth woman, who gets kicked in the face every now and then, but knows how to overcome, and how to laugh. She is intelligent, quick-witted, sharp, sarcastic, and puts men in their place like it's her job. "Leah Gardowski" can be considered a state of mind. We all have a little bit of Leah in us, but some of us just have more in common with her than others. You will be meeting Ms. Gardowski in section two. Actually, you won't be just meet her – you are going to become her (just for one section). You will get the chance to step into her shoes, and to experience different harsh, but undeniably humorous realities which are not uncommon of modern dating.

For me personally, the day I began to relate to Ms. Gardowski was the day I finally accepted that chick flicks lie. It was the day I learned that I just may have a higher likelihood of my tongue reaching my elbow than I do of finding "the one," and tying the knot. I realized I was quickly adding to my relationship roster, and that I had dated from a variety of backgrounds, a broad array of occupations, and even different states, to no avail. No, not "All My Exes Live in Texas," like George Strait's quirky hit song says, but I do in fact have one residing there and others in at least four different states (I'm honest about my story, unlike chick flicks). The realization of my near and far dating failures forced me to learn that the dating world is like a slot machine, or even to the extent of playing the lottery for some of us. You play until you win, just praying all the numbers will line up someday. Some get lucky right away. However, as time goes on, the unlucky typically feel exhausted from failed attempts and truly start to question their future in love.

First things first though. Today's dating realities aren't nearly as blissful as our dear chick flick fantasies. Hollywood sells us a love life of ball gowns, and roses and wine, while real life mostly brings us 9-5 dress clothes, fake flowers collecting dust, and our second cup of coffee for the day. Let's take a look at some of the cookie-cutter chick flick themes, and let's uncover the beautiful lies together, one step at a time.

20 CHICK FLICK LIES

Chick Flick Lie #1: Men catch cabs, steal cars, board trains, run down tarmacs, and jump on airplanes in mad pursuit of their woman.

Let's begin with the typical "happily ever after" ending. First of all though, the lead male has screwed up royally. He needs to win back his girl. What does he do? The classic daredevil chase, of course. He pulls a crazy, life-risking, law-breaking stunt all in the name of love. Not surprisingly, viewers ooh and ahh in absolute admiration of his relentless efforts. While this is one of the most popular chick flick endings, it is also one of the most unrealistic. Sorry to burst your bubble, friends. I know, I know. It is one of the most endearing to watch…I agree. (Okay, I said it. I'm a self-admitted sap, remember?)

Anyways, the breathtaking actor stops at nothing to get his girl back. He might catch the big city cab (most of us don't live in NYC), steal cars, board trains, chase subways, stop planes, and partake in every other crazy, daring stunt possible. While it's totally sweet to see a love-struck man dangling from a skyscraper holding up a "Will You Marry Me" or a "Please Forgive Me" sign while his lady is in an important company meeting in an all glass conference room at her job which is so much cooler than ours…it's not practical. Kacie in rural Montana has about a .00000000001% chance of this exact scenario happening to her, and she knows it.

It's true, ladies. Most men aren't going to stop a plane, run off their departing flight, risk their lives and those around them to catch up with the girl that's getting away. I don't know about you, but if there's a man out there who is willing to jump onto the wing of a plane to get his girl back…I haven't met him yet. I can't say I'd really expect a man to go that far, but thanks to Hollywood, I've entertained the idea that all of the above is quite possible.

The classic example of this dreamy scenario is the ending scene of "How to Lose a Guy in 10 days." Like a complete fantasy, Benjamin Barry (Matthew McConaughey) chases Andie Anderson (Kate Hudson), without any regard for his own life. Oh wait, it's not "like" a complete fantasy…it IS a complete fantasy. Has Matthew McConaughey or even his lookalike risked his life for you in busy traffic lately? Didn't think so. Anyways, on a motorcycle, Charming Ben recklessly weaves in and out of traffic in crazy pursuit of Andie. Since it's Hollywood, he does indeed catch up with the taxi, and Andie is of course stunned to see her "ex-whatever-he-is" outside her window. Of course she asks him if he's trying to get himself killed, to which he replies, "If that's what it takes…YEAH!….now pull over the cab!" After the driver pulls over, Ben faces Andie and tries to convince her she doesn't need to move to DC for a writing job. As his perfect hair blows in the wind, he tells her she can write anywhere, and he knows she's just running away. Of course for a split second, it appears Andie is rejecting him. Of course, she isn't REALLY rejecting him. Within seconds, the pair shares a passionate kiss, and Ben instructs the taxi driver to take her luggage home, because she has alternative transportation. Ohhhh…so many beautiful lies packed into one movie. Just the thought of the amazingly far-fetched outcome makes me want to pop in the DVD right here, right now…*Resisting the urge.*

The question is not how many of us women have daydreamed of a man doing something extra "out there" to express his undying love for us, but rather how many of us have NOT dreamed of this? In real life, the girl is more likely to go to DC for that job interview while the man sits at home. How about those other similar endings where man catches up with woman at airport? In real life, the man is more likely to drive away from the airport, while the woman he has just broken up with walks inside with mascara rolling down her cheeks. He typically drives home and leaves it at that, while she flies home...alone. He usually doesn't realize his mistake halfway home, or attempt a U-turn on a five lane interstate. He probably isn't going to go darting through security to beg for her forgiveness. So often in real life there aren't any turnarounds...only straight aheads. I know I'm a buzz kill here, but hey, I never promised to be anything else. You did read my "preface" and "introduction," right?

Chick Flick Lie #2: The public kiss with clapping bystanders.

Walking hand-in-hand with the athletic daredevil theme is the very public "happily-ever-after kiss" which usually takes place after guy catches up with girl, and lures her back in. We're on to you chick flicks...your endings include this very scenario 75% of the time. An award-winning kiss for a large applauding audience is classic and the good ole' standby type of chick flick ending. We all know how it goes in these films. The male character either apologizes for being an idiot or tells his lady that he forgives *her* errors. Different mistakes are made in different movies, but we all know the end result. He then proceeds to say a beautiful quote that you would almost never hear from a "real man." Not surprisingly, she forgives him, he picks her up, spins her around, and they share a public kiss which lasts longer than most real bride and groom smooches on their wedding day. The exhausted extras who have been on set all day doing this scene over and over again, still manage to cheer enthusiastically for the happy couple. Yes, it's fictional on so many levels. Nonetheless, I'm a sucker for this ending. I seriously love these.

The audience approved kiss takes place in countless chick flicks. Remember in "Hitch" when Mr. Hitch himself (Will Smith) chases down Sara (Eva Mendes)? Like McConaughey in chick flick lie #1, Smith risks his life for the one he loves. After Hitch gets thrown from the roof of Sara's car and injures himself, she frantically asks: "Are you trying to get yourself killed?" His response? "If that's what it takes!" Woah, woah...wait a minute. Isn't that the SAME exact question and reply which occurred during McConaughey's crazy stunt with Kate Hudson? Yes, it is folks. Two of the greatest chick flicks in history sell the idea that Mr. Right will confess his love to you for everyone and their brother to hear, and put his life on the line in the process.

We also see the classic public make-out session in "Maid in Manhattan," "The Wedding Planner," "The Proposal," "A Cinderella Story," and "New in Town," among so many others. "Never Been Kissed" has perhaps the biggest clapping bystander kiss in the history of all Hollywood romances. As Sam Coulson (Michael Vartan) gives Josie Geller (Drew Barrymore) her first kiss on the baseball field, the crowd roars with support. This just might be kind of an unusual setting for your *first kiss ever*, huh?

The question is not which chick flicks feature the PDA ending, but rather, which ones do not? It's so beautifully pathetically unrealistic, yet so incredibly fun to daydream about. This ending shows how in love two people can be. Real love isn't afraid to let the world know. Time stands still, and they do not care about who is watching, or what they're thinking. It's just the two of them in that moment, and it gives off the impression that their relationship will last forever. Okay, I'm getting carried away here. Moving on...

Chick Flick Lie #3: Nice guys always win in the end.

Okay, so let's continue the list of lies with the classic theme which is the concluding result in almost every chick flick...no matter what the plot is. The exception to the typical is that in some chick flicks the woman ends up with no one because of a death or some other rare unforeseen circumstance. However, we can rest assured that in the cinema, no big screened sweetheart will ever end up with a jerk at the end. Nice guys simply don't lose in Hollywood. Let's face it. Sure, the man she rides off into the sunset with may not have been the greatest guy during the beginning and middle of the movie, but at the end, he's a flawless poet. That's just how it rolls in Hollywood, folks. A majority of the time though, he was a likable character, and the nice guy from the get-go. Yes, in most cases, viewers seemingly fall in love with his expressive, caring demeanor within the 30 seconds of the film. Either way though, chick flicks send the message that the right man always walks away with the right girl. Yes, the movie ends how we want normally, with the good guy getting the girl. She chooses the guy we all root for all along. We may have even shouted at the screen for her to do so.

One of the greatest silver screen scenarios of the nice guy winning the girl is undoubtedly "The Wedding Singer." Julia Sullivan (Drew Barrymore) is originally engaged to the worst of the worst. Her fiancé Glenn Gulia (Matthew Glave) is a shameless cheater. However, the "nice guy," Robbie Hart (Adam Sandler), is the one who steals Julia's heart in the end.

Countless other movies feature love triangles, and the main character struggling to choose between two very different men. Now, don't get me wrong – sometimes the man who ends up on the losing end isn't exactly horrible. Sometimes the scriptwriters don't make "the loser" all that bad of a guy. However, the "nicer" guy is always slightly more likable to viewers and to the girl. Consequently, he will always walk away with her in the end.

Interestingly, even though the nice guy always winning is a classic Hollywood lie, I have found that it is perhaps the best lesson teacher of all chick flicks. Hear me out here: The nice guy SHOULD win in real life too.

Now imagine for a minute, if she ever chose the guy who was a complete, unwilling to change, jerk…We would be completely outraged if she chose the undeserving man in the end, wouldn't we?

We would toss our empty popcorn buckets at the rolling credits and the commentary would go something like this:

"WHAT!? That was like the worst movie I've ever seen in my entire life!"

"Is she stupid? It was obvious who the better guy was!"

"I'm seriously so disappointed. I didn't expect that!"

No matter how you state it, we would carry on and on about how awful it was. Wait a second though: So many of us so often seal that fate for ourselves in real life. Yes…yes we do, whether we want to admit it or not. Sadly, in a non-fiction event, many of us would choose the jerk if we were in her shoes, despite the fact that we don't root for him to end up with her. Well…welcome to reality. In Hollywood, when a woman is torn between two men, one of which is a jerk and one of which is a sweetheart, she is definitely going to choose the sweetheart. In real life? Nine times out of ten, ladies are going to run straight into the arms of the undeserving man, leaving the deserving one in shambles. There are countless exceptions…I know, I know.

What about you, missy? Are you struggling over a guy who your friends are continually trying to convince you is a jerk or not worth your time? Are they always telling you that you are beautiful, amazing, and deserve so much better? Still, he's the guy you want and you've made every excuse for him in the book? Do you hear me now? Think of your life like these films. In the same way you don't want the beautiful amazing character to end up with the jerk…don't seal that fate for yourself, and don't sell yourself short. Staying stuck on an undeserving clown isn't the ideal ending for her…and isn't for you. Any movie where a woman ends up with the jerk would undoubtedly receive horrific reviews from the critics. **Just a thought:** *Aren't we also choosing a horrific awful ending in real life if we choose the undeserving man who doesn't appreciate us? Are we setting the standards higher for the character than we* *are for ourselves? Are we choosing "crappily ever after" when we only want to watch "happily ever after?"*

Chick Flick Lie #4: The bad boy gone good: Liars no longer lie, cheaters no longer cheat, and everyone lives happily ever after.

Along the same lines of the nice guy winning, is the bad boy gone good. This lie may sound like a contradiction after reading #3, but hear me out for a second. Remember, a guy might not start out as a stand-up character in every flick, but by the end, he's volunteering in soup kitchens and working to save the world. By the end, he is a "VERY nice guy." This theme is perhaps my favorite Hollywood message of all time. Perhaps, I love the bad boy gone good storyline so much because I've been good at finding bad boys and bad at finding good boys. I must confess these particular movies fill me up with an awesome message of false hope for my dysfunctional situations. If it's a fire and gasoline relationship movie, I'm admittedly going to be super glued to the screen. I won't even be aimlessly scrolling through my iPhone, or talking to the person next to me...I will instead be taking in the falsifications on the screen in front of me, and comparing the storyline to my past relationships. Despite the bad boy to good boy transformation we often see in this type of Chick Flick, reality strongly begs to differ.

In the best chick flicks that utilize this storyline however, the bad boy often has an epiphany or an astounding moment of truth in which he decides to ditch his bad habits whether it is laziness, binge drinking or extreme womanizing. He suddenly gives up his multiple women for one woman whom he loves more than he does being an addict or a player. His cheating and lying ways come to an end, because his new one and only makes him want to change for the better. The once untrustworthy skirt chaser decides he wants to be monogamous. The scriptwriters make him a brand new man...one of instant integrity, who the audience helplessly falls for. Chick flicks are incredible at mastering the falsehood that liars no longer lie, cheaters no longer cheat, and everyone lives happily ever after.

One of the movies I believe ultimately illustrates this lie is "Ghosts of Girlfriends Past." Once again, heartthrob Matthew McConaughey is the charming leading man. In this particular film, he is a champion womanizer with a strategic playbook. He goes through women faster than he does boxers. However, in the end, ladies' man Connor Mead (McConaughey) exclusively settles down with Jennifer Garner (Jenny Perotti), the one girl whom he's always loved. While she is initially skeptical of his "changed ways," she decides he is being sincere, and she gives in. In this movie, it all appears so genuine and so real. It's as if Connor has become a new man.

People change, right? Well, of course this kind of thing does happen in real life and it's an encouraging possibility to keep in mind. We should never minimize that with God all things are possible. Since he never stops believing in us despite all of our shortcomings, we shouldn't stop believing in others either…BUT the man has to allow the Lord to work in his heart and legitimately want to change. No one can make the decision for change except the man himself…for he is given free will. Though there are indeed exceptions in the "bad boy gone good" concept, realize it is unfortunately more often that people stay the same, rather than legitimately step outside their comfort zone and change their ways.

I'm going to give it to you straight: If a man has cheated on you, there is an excellent chance he will do so again. Likewise, if a man has lied to you, there is a massive chance he will do so again, and again, and again. In real life, if you accept true mistreatment, you invite it to continue. If you reject mistreatment and vow to not settle for anything less than you deserve, you will be opening the door to meeting someone new and deserving of your heart.

The brutal moving on process becomes even tougher when Hollywood paints the perfect picture of the player who turns into the "one woman man boyfriend of the year. Let us not forget the compulsive liar who reverts to "Honest Henry." Then the credits roll and an audience of female viewers exit the theatre with a sparkle in their eyes. These awestruck women are hoping that maybe the man who is currently disappointing them will change…just like the man in the inspiring film they just paid $10 to be encouraged by.

Let us remember that in the movies, it is easy for the story to end so well because:

1. It is a movie.
2. Happily ever after is a movie thing. In real life, it is a non-existent conclusion which people do not actually get to experience, as there is so much more work to be done than what a movie shows. What the movies don't show you is a "Two years later follow up" when "Mr. Cheater" returns to his cheating ways, or "Mr. I Love to Lie" returns to his lack of honesty character.

Since our lives are not the movies, there is a beginning, middle, and an end to every revitalized relationship that was once deeply troubled. Don't get me wrong…the end could result in 50 years of a Christ-centered, loyal, happy marriage. However, in real life "Mr. So- Called Changed Man" is so often likely to relapse instead of adhere to his supposable lifestyle change. The violation may be with his secretary, his stylist, or his ex, but rest assured, he is likely to offend again. We have minutes, days, weeks, months, and years to overcome and to stay faithful throughout. Happily ever after doesn't show the effort it takes or the true struggle that continues after the reunited couple gives it another try.

I too fell into the trap (more than once) that I could change a bad boy and failed miserably. It seems as if I'm not alone with my struggles in this area, because many women seem to have the same attraction to the same trap. I can confidently say I am not the only woman who can be deemed as a "project seeker." Maybe it's the challenge that comes with falling in love with a bad boy? Maybe there is just something sexy about him? Maybe it's the potential we see in him, because we think we see a diamond in the rough? No matter what it is that makes women take interest in the bad news boy, they usually fall deeply in love with him, and go along for the crazy ride that goes with him. We all know how this usually plays out in real life, despite what the movies tell us. Someone usually does "change," and sadly it's often the good girl, instead of the bad boy. However, the chick flicks paint such an attractive picture that makes the transition so easy to believe in.

Again, please do not misunderstand me…the "great change" CAN happen, but realize it more often does NOT happen. This is what I mean by positive pessimism, friends: You are pessimistic that he is going to just automatically do a 180, BUT you are positive that you are going to be okay either way.

Chick Flick Lie #5: Massive betrayals are easily forgiven and forgotten…No problem!

Has anyone else noticed the classic theme in which an earth-shaking betrayal is quickly forgiven and forgotten? One fast and easy apology and everything returns to hunky-dory, right? Now, let me be clear. We should all practice forgiveness for sure…It is biblical that we forgive. It is healthy for our hearts and our well-being. Refusal to forgive and harboring bitterness is undoubtedly toxic, and will ensure a miserable life. However, in reality, the average person isn't exactly going to just brush off being the victim of a serious deception, forget the whole entire betrayal, and go running straight back into the arms of the traitor.

Need a specific example to grasp what I'm sharing here? Easy! If you've been watching chick flicks for any period of time, you have most likely seen the journalist plot, in which someone's new "romantic interest" uses them for a major news story without their permission. C'mon you know you've watched it at least once, and it was so predictable. The ground-breaking, earth-shaking story runs, and it is spread around the world. It is a complete success for the news outlet and of course the man in charge. However, it is a complete embarrassment for the victim, and brings an overbearing sense of guilt for the writer. As the script usually goes, the struggling writer is offered the promotion they have dreaming of…but it took betraying their new interest in the process. Their love prospect finds out they are the subject of a not so flattering news piece, and goes storming out of the room. The split takes place, and they appear doomed. However, in Hollywood the victim always ends up forgiving (as they should), forgetting (I wouldn't do that), and everything is suddenly peachy keen (what are they thinking?). Have you figured out I'm talking about "27 Dresses" here?

However, "27 Dresses" is a far cry from the only offender in this category. "How to Lose a Guy in 10 Days" features a similar plot. Yes ladies, some of our favorite chick flicks tell multiple lies within one film. What about "While You Were Sleeping," in which Lucy (Sandra Bullock) lied about being engaged to Peter Callaghan (Peter Gallagher) for a good part of the movie? Of course though, viewers are drawn to sweet Lucy, and they are definitely rooting for her. Once Lucy's big lie is revealed, not only does the family soon forgive her, but they also support her quickly marrying Peter's brother Jack (Bill Pullman), whom she fell for while Peter was sleeping.

Let's return to the liars no longer lying once again: What about the movies in which he lies about his job? She lies about her background? Someone lies about their family, their age, their credit card debt, etc. etc. No matter what the case, all is forgiven and forgotten on the silver screen. They make up and out in front of a large crowd on a busy sidewalk. The victim now completely trusts the betrayer, and it's as if the sellout never ever happened.

Now, in real life…these betrayals would almost certainly be the end of that relationship. The person wouldn't get a second swing after strike one. It would be a good-bye, so-long, adios, farewell……and would also include a Facebook unfriend and a Twitter un-follow sort of thing.

Hmmm…maybe you should take back that guy who built your entire relationship on lies for two years? Imagine you're a chick flick with the perfect ending…can't you see the credits rolling now?

As good as this happy ending makes the heart feel, oftentimes in life the reconciliation moment doesn't happen. Sometimes they really just walk away only to never return. Sometimes a man doesn't forgive the woman who destroyed his career. Sometimes the woman can't take back the guy who has lied to her all the way back to the first date. Unlike the ending of our favorite chick flicks, some mistakes are fatal and final.

Chick Flick Lie #6: The "ugly duckling" transforms into a beautiful swan.

Sometimes the truth hurts and this is one of those unfortunate times. Hollywood is quite the master of instantly turning the repulsive "ugly duckling" who men avoid like the plague into a desirable swan princess. As revealed in the opening introduction, the "ugly duckling" has a hideous style. She dresses like she's about 40 years older than she actually is, her glasses are dated, and her hair is pulled back in a tight bun. If you ever notice though, there is ALWAYS potential behind the glasses. She also usually has a fit physique…the kind someone can only get from working out consistently. However, that isn't exactly acknowledged or spotlighted until her transformation is revealed. We aren't exactly led to believe that the seemingly clumsy, uncoordinated girl does "CrossFit" or "Insanity" like it's her job…but evidently the actress does.

The unforgettable flick, "She's All That" masters the ugly duckling theme. Zack Siler (Freddie Prinze Jr.) is the big man on campus, while Laney Boggs (Rachael Leigh Cook) is known as the dorky unpopular girl. Though Zack initially started wooing Laney and trying to transform her into a prom queen as part of a bet, he predictably winds up developing true feelings for her. Of course Laney is furious when she realizes she was the subject of a bet, but ultimately forgives and ends up with him in the end (also further validating lie #5). "My Big Fat Greek Wedding" also showcases the unlikely girl scoring the unlikely guy. Toula (Nia Vardalos) scores the handsome Ian Miller (John Corbett) shortly after she undergoes a makeover and starts a new job.

This Hollywood transformation often goes something like this: Suddenly, the coke bottle glasses come off. Her style goes from ultra conservative to Vegas nightlife in 2.5 seconds, and she snags the hottest guy on planet earth. Of course he often first notices her behind the glasses though. Her inner beauty and brains is what originally attracted him, right? C'mon people! How often does the stereotyped straight-laced antique suit wearing lady score the city's most eligible bachelor? Don't get me wrong here...she SO should...because the woman I am speaking of here is intelligent, intriguing, and has an amazing heart... but sadly, men don't always pick a woman based on her heart. I'll admit when many women are looking at a man, they often place the importance of outer over inner as well. Sadly, both sexes can be quite shallow in this area. Though this way of thinking isn't right – it's still often a reality. Now, I'm not saying this common Hollywood scenario has never happened in real life. I am however saying that so often the ugly personality with the pretty face wins out simply due to the laws of physical attraction. Thankfully though, I somehow still believe anyone who has a true desire to find someone will eventually be paired up with the one who sees them as beautiful. Different people have different definitions of beauty. One man's cup of tea may not be another's man... and that's good. We're only intended to end up with one person in end...not multiple...Okay...moving right along...

Chick Flick Lie #7: The man who sings outside your window.

Ohhhhh, this one hits home! Does it ever! Why? Well, because I live in Music City USA, where you would think this sort of thing would happen...and ya know, it probably does happen to some women...but not to me. Seriously though, it's one of the cutest chick flick scenes ever. I'm a sucker for out of tune movie singers...I can't deny it, and I just can't hide it.

You know what I mean: "Colton" starts seeing this adorable girl, but somewhere in between he messes up royally, and she walks away from him. He then has to try his hardest to win her back. What's he do? He sings a song outside her window confessing his mad love for her of course. He's quite the writer and quite the master of smoothing things over, because "Forgiving Felicia" decides to take him back. In most movies, the "Coltons" are out of tune…unless of course they are playing a musician, in which case, they are perfect, just like the ending.

"A lot Like Love" starring Oliver Martin (Ashton Kutcher) and Emily Friehl (Amanda Peet) illustrates this chick flick lie in the most beautiful fashion possible. After many years of a dysfunctional on again and off again fling, Oliver heads to Emily's house with his guitar and sings her a song. He sings it loud, and he sings it proud. Her nearby neighbors all clap in approval. Unfortunately, Emily was engaged at this point in the movie, and they would have to endure a few more chapters before their happily ever after. The ending of "Music & Lyrics" is also a woman's dream come true. Alex Fletcher (Hugh Grant), a former pop star, realizes he messed up royally with his soul mate lover and co-writer, Sophie Fisher (Drew Barrymore). What's he do? Well, at a sold out show, in which he is performing alongside the world's biggest pop star, he gets the chance to sing a song of his own. While playing the piano, the handsome Alex sings the original "Don't Write Me Off," to Sophie who is in the massive audience. Of course her eyes well up with tears, and of course, this moving song is enough to win her back.

Has anyone out there had a man try to smooth things over by singing to them in a public place, or at the least, has anyone had a man try to serenade them while they stand outside on their balcony? If so, congratulations lucky girl!

Chick Flick Lie #8: Beautiful poetic quotes from the most unlikely men.

As much as women love to have the best of both worlds (and some of us certainly do have that), let us remind ourselves that a vast majority of us will never have that "perfection" in our relationships. What I'm speaking of here is the football star who is ALSO an aspiring poet. C'mon now...it's usually one or the other, but in Hollywood, you get BOTH in any given movie. The guy plays football like a rising Brett Favre, is an honor student, volunteers at the mission, and is as expressive as Shakespeare. He says the most profound things...he's just perfect. He may be surrounded by a locker room full of foul-mouthed men who are constantly counting the notches on their belts, but this guy? He's instead writing poetry for the woman of his dreams. He knows how to balance both worlds. His Dad wants him to play football professionally, but he wants to write. Don't you just love all the beautiful, too good to be true quotes that come from his perfect lips?

This scenario puts me in mind of "A Cinderella Story" starring Hillary Duff and Chad Michael Murray. Though my description isn't completely identical to the entire storyline of this movie, it bares much resemblance. The dreams of Sam Montgomery (Duff) come true when she realizes her expressive internet love is none other than football star Austin Ames (Murray). Though Austin and Sam have their rough patches, he leaves a crucial play in the game with nine seconds on the clock, to go kiss his princess in front of the whole entire stadium instead. Of course the rain also starts pouring at the most opportune time. He then goes on to live his writing dreams with Sam. They go to Princeton instead of where his daddy wanted him to go. Don't you just love this perfect ending? Of course you do...we all do...and we can thank Hollywood for the unrealistic expectations which have resulted from this!

Chick Flick Lie #9: Slow motion running and the quick turnaround.

So simple, but so sweet, is the slow motion run, brought to us by our favorite unrealistic romantic movies. The soon-to-be forever couple shows up at the same location, and then one or the other, or both, spots the other, and their open armed love run which is slower than molasses causes viewers to gush and grab their tissues. After what feels like a Guinness World Records' journey, the perfect couple shares that picture perfect kiss which also gives the latest kissing record a run for its money. Wow, Hollywood, you really had us fooled into thinking this one was going to have a heartbreaking ending. Thanks for reaffirming that a chick flick ALWAYS has a blissful, unrealistic conclusion. You seriously had us thinking otherwise for a second.

Then there's the famous "quick turnaround," which usually takes place during the PDA portion of the movie, but it can take place in any kind of ending really. The quick turnaround occurs when the movie looks like it's going to end up as anything but happy. It looks as though prince charming is going to be turned down. It looks as though he isn't going to be forgiven. His dream girl just isn't accepting his apology, and she likely even starts to walk away. She's just not buying his "I will change my ways" talk…but then, he says just the right thing. Something profound and something deeply meaningful comes out of his mouth, and it is just enough for him to get out of the ten foot hole he had previously dug himself into. The "quick turnaround" can also be the man who chases the plane down the tarmac only to lose it. He thinks his girl has officially got away, but then he turns around, and BAM… there she is. The quick turnaround is most definitely one of the silver screen's favorite tactics. They try to trick us, but we all know it is going to end well no matter what.

On the woman's side of trying to win back the man, I think of "Win a Date with Tad Hamilton." Rosalee Futch (Kate Bosworth) realizes her mistake of rejecting the love of lifelong friend Pete Monash (Topher Grace), because she now has a newfound relationship with celebrity Tad Hamilton (Josh Duhamel). Pete tries to stop Rosalee from leaving town with Tad, but he fails. Since Rosalee reciprocates Pete's love, she doesn't feel confident in her choice. It is now her job to make things right…and make things right, she does. You see, Pete is leaving town and transferring jobs now that he's lost the girl he loves. However, one can assume by the end of the film, he'll stay put.

It's a rainy night and Rosalee catches up with him. She drives up beside him to alert him and catches him off guard, because he's currently all doom and gloom flipping through sad stuff on the radio. After Pete goes off the road and gets into a minor crash, the two get out of their vehicles to face one another. They very slowly walk towards one another and then stop, still leaving a great deal of space in between the two of them. There aren't any hugs or affectionate greetings at this point. For a good bit, they are silent, and both at a loss for words. Rosalee gives him a cute line about his five smiles, but Pete doesn't immediately respond in the way she wants. He stands there with a long pause and then says, "I can't believe I'm going to say this but…" Of course Rosalee's face shows that she assumes the worst, and of course viewers are on the edge of their seats. Then he finishes his cliffhanger sentence with "Would you like to dance?" (The radio just so happens to send a song out to all the lovers out there). Then you know how it ends…all kiss and bliss.

In real life, the quick turnaround seldom happens. I know…sad, right? People usually take much more time to think than what is shown. They usually don't push away and then pull in their lover's face for a passionate kiss all within a one minute period. In reality, sometimes a man simply doesn't give in to the change of heart woman who previously pushed him away for another man. Sometimes "no" really means "no" and "over" really means "over."

Chick Flick Lie #10: The dateless bridesmaid ends up with a date by the end of the night.

The lonely bridesmaid who magically ends up with a date by the end of the night is another common write we see in a chick flick script. Whether she is simply a bridesmaid or the maid of honor, she probably did a majority of the planning. In fact, we can probably go as far as to call her the "overworked bridesmaid." She is looking as glamorous as the bride, but she is sitting alone. She is watching the happy couples around her, and being harshly reminded of her singleness all night. She flashes that gentle but sad little half smile at the bride and groom wishing she had what they had. Her eyes say it all.

Not to fret though, because in a movie, this scenario usually results in a happy ending:

A) She either meets someone at the wedding…or
B) The man she loves shows up just in time. You know, it's a "may I have this dance?" kind of moment.

Yes friends, I have an example of both A and B for you. An example of scenario A would be the movie "Hitch." Yes, this classic flick contains some great illustrations for my debunking quest in more ways than one. Remember the jaded Casey Sedgewick (Julie Ann Emery), who had lost hope in men? Well, at the end of the movie while attending Allegra and Albert's wedding, she meets a possible Mr. Right. She is sitting at the reception alone when an elderly woman pretends she is choking. Casey jumps right in to help. The elderly wing woman then praises her for "saving her life." Next, enters her gorgeous grandson who thanks Casey for helping his dear sweet grandma. It was all a scheme orchestrated by granny. The smiles we see on the faces of the two dateless people insinuate a future in the making. Casey didn't have to endure the reception alone after all!

Example B? Definitely "The Wedding Date." Nick Mercer (Dermot Mulroney) was initially going to be the wedding date of Kat Ellis (Debra Messing). However, some serious drama transpires, which causes what seems like irreparable conflict between them. Nick even heads to the airport to leave town, but decides he needs to be back at the wedding with Kat. Of course he shows up at the wedding, reclaims his date, ends up being the best man and all is well in the world again.

Listen single ladies…in real life, sometimes we have to suck it up and get through that wedding, be happy for the new couple, and enjoy the day dateless. Sometimes all you can do is remind yourself that someday you will have a handsome date of your own on your arm. Better yet, someday your best friend will be attending YOUR wedding to the man of your dreams. Yes, when you arrive without a date, you typically have to suck it up and get through that wedding alone. Sometimes you've got to watch everyone else dance and suck faces on the dance floor, and remind yourself that if you desire to be married, your day is coming too.

Even more importantly though, you should enjoy the moment…as a single lady. Don't rob yourself of the here and now. There is beauty in your current freedom. God has reasons for it and good ones. You can dance with whomever you want at these events (so long as he isn't someone else's man). When they call the "single ladies" to the floor for the bouquet toss, strut on up there with confidence, and enjoy your spotlighted moment. Heck, start a collection of the bouquets you catch. Maybe you will catch more than the average woman and be able to break a world record…you just never know, sister!

Chick Flick Lie #11: Background music.

Have you ever wished life had background music like they do in the movies for all the important scenes? I know I have. Wouldn't it especially be nice if danger music existed? It would sound something like John Williams' "Jaws" warning music every time you meet a player or a creepy stalker. In contrast, if you actually ran across a decent man, it would sound something like Mendelssohn's "Wedding March," or Pachelbel's "Canon in D."

How about that amazingly beautiful opera music in "Pretty Woman"…you know, the La Traviata – Amami Alfredo? As stunning Edward Lewis (Richard Gere) pulls up in a gorgeous limo to rescue his beloved Vivian Ward (Julia Roberts), this heavenly music is blaring. Of course she is on the top floor, and of course he calls her "Princess Vivian." Like a sexy superhero or just a really brave Prince Charming with flowers in his mouth, Edward takes his umbrella and uses it to pull down that rickety ladder, and makes his way up to the love of his life.

Face-to-face he asks her "So what happened after he climbed up the tower and rescued her?"

Vivian replies, "She rescues him right back." Awe! Where are the tissues, friends?

As we know all too well, in any movie, not just chick flicks, there is background music to set the tone. Not only could we be more "aware" of what is happening if background music existed in real life, but it would add a little pizazz to the day in, day out stuff every now and then, wouldn't it?

Chick Flick Lie #12: Prince Charming waits at the bottom of a beautiful red-carpeted stairwell.

Ahh..have you ever watched those flicks in which a flawless woman walks out in her gorgeous evening gown, and her ridiculously handsome prince is waiting for her at the bottom of the stairs? Think Titanic - Jack Dawson (Leonardo DiCaprio) and Rose DeWitt Bukater (Kate Winslet), style. He's got stars in his eyes, and he is so taken up with her every step. When she gets to the bottom of the stairs, he extends his hand, she gives it to him, and he gently kisses it. Yeah, that's a lie too, girls.

It's too bad that in real life the closest thing to a reenactment of this scenario is running down those steps at your apartment complex. You may see a cutie waiting for you and smiling at you from the bottom of the steps, but it's really because the stairwell isn't wide enough for you to pass one another. To top it all off, you're too crushed over your recent breakup to actually talk to him, and you're in a huge hurry. You tell yourself he's just being polite, and you're praying to God that you don't tumble down those stairs. In real life, you're not at the ball and neither is he. However, it is casual Friday, and you're both on your way to work. He's waiting to run back upstairs because he forgot something. There's no beautiful carpeting on those steps either, but there is mud, and possibly some "dog stuff" smeared on there, which you've got to avoid stepping in. How's that for reality?

Chick Flick Lie #13: The in-laws' dislike for one another is easily resolved.

Family conflicts being magically resolved before the credits roll is another classic phenomenon in Hollywood. I can never get over the quick fixes in the films where the in-laws who strongly disliked one another throughout the entire movie, suddenly very easily and willingly set their differences aside for good. Different scenarios apply to different flicks. It could be that the adjoining families don't like one another. The bride's parents detest the groom's parents perhaps. Commonly the dad doesn't initially like his daughter's fiancé, but rest assured, within a couple of hours, he will love his son-in-law. Everyone will love everyone. Usually the scrutinized character does something heroic which wins over their critic. Before we know it, the marital blessings are given, the vows are exchanged, the day runs perfectly from start to finish, and everyone is a happy camper.

Take "Guess Who" for example. Percy Jones (Bernie Mac) couldn't have been less of a fan of his daughter's boyfriend Simon Green (Ashton Kutcher). By the end of the movie, however, the two decided they were best pals.

What about "Monster-In-Law" with Viola Fields (Jane Fonda), and Charlotte 'Charlie' Cantilini (Jennifer Lopez)? Viola stopped at nothing to destroy Charlotte's relationship with her son Dr. Kevin Fields (Michael Vartan). What happened in the grand finale though? You guessed it - Viola realizes she does want Charlotte as her daughter-in-law, and she agrees to an attitude adjustment.

Another movie which demonstrates this classic theme? Definitely "You Again." Marni Olivia Olsen (Kristen Bell) completely loses her marbles upon finding out that her brother Will (James Wolk) is engaged to (Joanna 'J-J- Clark (Odette Annable). Marni's high school experience was extra rough thanks to mean girl Joanna. However, now that Joanna is about to marry into the family, she pretends she doesn't remember Marni. The plot thickens when we are introduced to Joanna's aunt who raised her. Ramona 'Mona' Clark (Sigourney Weaver) just happens to be the former high school arch nemesis of Will and Marni's mother, Gail Byer Olsen (Jamie Lee Curtis). With the two families uniting, Marni will not be the only one enduring a difficult acceptance process. After physical altercations, injuries, conniving schemes, and trying to ruin one another's lives, everyone decides to put their differences aside in the end. Well, almost. At the wedding reception, Will and Marni's dearest Grandma Bunny (Betty White) is introduced to Joanna's grandma, who just happens to be her old high school rival Helen (Cloris Leachman). Time certainly hasn't erased the hard feelings, and Grandma Bunny steals the man who Helen is wanting to dance with. Talk about an ongoing family competition! Nonetheless, Will and Joanna wind up happily married without any true family tension. C'mon now... seriously? Nonetheless, I LOVE this movie.

It would be great if all the above examples were typical of real life, and perhaps these types of chick flicks represent how accepting we should actually be (if the couple is happy and the relationship is healthy, of course). However, how often do these scenarios actually happen? Sure most parents or siblings "come around" and set their reservations aside when the marriage officially happens, because they know they need to for their loved one's sake. However, let us never forget that the movies once again fail to show us that "Two years later follow-up" where conflict is brewing once again. The couple's parents are in competition for the "Grandparents of the Year Award" now that the first child has been born. Maybe Dad detests his son-in-law more than ever because of his refusal to get a job to provide for his daughter and grandchild. Perhaps the overbearing mother-in-law has returned, and she tells her son and daughter-in-law how to decorate their house, and raise their children. Then there's this: The sister and her sister-in-law are back in intense competition, driving the man in the middle crazy. Basically these real life couples could quite possibly be on the brink of divorce. Okay, so it'd be nice if that weren't reality...but it so often is.

Chick Flick Lie #14: Most singles live in high rise buildings and have prestigious jobs.

Speaking of the glamorizing which takes place in the moviemaking business, who else kind of wishes they worked in a 28 story building overlooking a beautiful view of the city? Not only do most chick flicks showcase the perfect dating relationship or the perfect ending to all love stories, but they often showcase the prestigious career in a dreamy location (unless of course she is the underdog, which might be the case in 30% of movies). If she isn't the underdog like Annie Walker (Kristen Wiig) in "Bridesmaids," she is definitely the corporate hot shot. Yes, there are exceptions, folks. A majority of our classic love stories choose one of the two themes, but usually they take the rich route. Seldom is there an in between.

I can't help but love how movies so often paint the picture of a high profile career and an upscale high rise apartment, even though love and life supposedly aren't going the way that the character had planned. These movies feature fancy elevators, briefcases, dreamy promotions, perfectly pressed designer suits, gorgeous hair and amazing makeup. They boast spacious offices and hold their professional meetings in all glass conference rooms. Believe it or not, not all of us live in a big city, work in skyscraper buildings and have the careers of journalists, CEOS and fashion designers.

In real life, it is quite possible that a true-to-life heartbroken woman instead works as a receptionist for the small, run down, one level local automotive shop. She probably wears dress casual clothes at best (which she probably has trouble affording), uses a recycled tin can as her pencil holder, in which she grabs a pencil from to throw back her severely split-ended hair that has needed a trim for the past three months. Oh, and she simply didn't feel like wearing her contacts this morning. Not to mention, her alarm clock didn't go off. So, it's instead a no makeup, glasses, messy bun and running late kind of day.

Real life is also a messy, average apartment. Even my little brother, who barely watches chick flicks pointed out that most films include a beautiful home or an elaborate high rise apartment. Whether or not you're a city gal, aren't those penthouses with a million dollar view something else? Not only do these fairy tale movies contain expensive housing, but with few exceptions, they even eat in unusually upscale restaurants with valet, drive above average fancy cars, and like I said, they have high class jobs to top it all off. Seriously, I want to know where all of the out-of-this-world fancy restaurants actually exist. Even as someone who lives in the city of Nashville, I can say we definitely have some restaurants we consider fancy and upscale, but they usually still don't compare to what we see on the silver screen. Oh, and most of us can't exactly afford to eat at those places every day. You don't exactly see the characters in these movies ordering off the dollar board menus, now do you?

Also, girlfriends in the movies always get to talk over manicures, pedicures, and full- fledged spa days. Their relaxing heart-to-heart talks make heartbreak look more tolerable. In real life, girlfriend comes to your messy place or you go to hers, and you use the little cash you have to buy you some generic brand ice cream from the grocery store, or you grab your half eaten one out of the freezer. Then you proceed to cry together. You just may even spare a dollar or two to rent a chick flick from Redbox.

Chick Flick Lie #15: Long Distance Relationships magically work out

As aforementioned, these addictive cinematic creations we all fall victim to, love to present us with the "quick fix" approaches. Along with the cheaters who quit cheating, the liars who stop lying, and the feuding in-laws who wind up loving one another, long distance relationships also magically work themselves out. By the end of the film, one person is giving up their career in a different state, turning down an attractive promotion, or the couple confidently makes plans for the day when they can be in the same continent. We hear the "I've never been more sure of anything in my life," line in this type of movie.

"Letters to Juliet" presents us with this beautiful lie in the most beautiful way. In this fairy tale, Sophie (Amanda Seyfried) falls in love with a London boy named Charlie (Christopher Egan), while on a vacation with her annoying fiancé. You know how the story goes. A complicated love triangle begins, and for a while, it looks as though there isn't any hope for Sophie and Charlie. As the movies would have it, Sophie breaks off her engagement and heads back to London. Charlie finds her standing on the balcony (how cliché), and climbs up to get her (again, how cliché). Nonetheless, it's cute, it's sweet, and it's the perfect escape from reality. Charlie expresses his mad love for Sophie, and suggests they flip on where they're going to live. He will leave London in a heartbeat if that is what Sophie wants. Yeahhhhh…

Okay, long distance relationships can certainly work in real life (happens all the time) if a couple is strong enough, but has anyone else continually failed at long distance relationships? Has anyone decided what continent they're going to live in by the flipping of a coin? Does anyone else think the movies make it look way too easy? If so, raise your hand so that I don't feel left out here. If you ask me, long distance relationships are among the toughest relationships to be in. "The out of sight out of mind" worry is a constant one, as are travel expenses (unless you're rich like the characters in most movies). Ohhh, and who has upteen hours of vacation time for use? Sorry folks, I know this one is written like a true pessimist, but long distance hasn't been my friend on more than one occasion. In chick flicks though, all the big problems which go with this sort of relationship just fade away as the credits roll. Oh well, good for them....I suppose!

Chick Flick Lie #16: Successful big city girl comes back to her old small town where she is reunited with her old flame…who is still single at 35.

Another typical chick flick story line is the successful big city girl who takes a trip down memory lane by going back to the gossipy small town she was raised in for an impromptu visit. Think "Hope Floats" and "Sweet Home Alabama" style. The leading lady is beautiful, as driven as they come, and her social standing is phenomenal. However, she puts on a façade and tries her hardest to mirror who everyone thinks she is these days. If it isn't enough that she has to come back home with her head held high somehow, she tries her best to walk every step with the utmost perfection, and she also has to face the past in the midst of serious relationship drama. Perhaps she even has to run into her high school arch nemesis again. She will likely face criticism and judgment from her old community. She may have treated someone like crap who now has two kids and a baby on the way, or she may be faced with the girl whose weight she once poked fun at. On the other hand, she may have to reunite with the mean girl who tried to ruin her life.

Usually in these types of themes, something hurtful brings her back home whether it is a divorce, an ill family member, a funeral, a wedding, etc. She's almost always come a looooong ways since those small town days. However, there is one important aspect of her life that is not going so well: Her love life. Every piece of her life seems to fall into place except "love," and unfortunately this missing component is huge to her, and undoubtedly has caused an unhappiness that can no longer be fulfilled by her career achievements.

You know what happens in the movie next, right? Her high school love (the one that got away) just happens to still be single, and they have the same magical connection they had back in the day. Now that they're older adults with a new set of responsibilities, there will be some obstacles they have to face, but in the end, they will overcome and end up living happily ever after. Sounds adorable, doesn't it? I agree, but this is yet another scenario I have admittedly lived…minus the blissful ending. For me, it started out like "The Notebook," but ended more like the "Amityville Horror."

Of course this kind of thing does happen in real life though. No matter where life takes a successful person, "home" and the people there always remain in their heart. However, how often is your old high school flame still single and kid-less in your small town at the age of 35? C'mon, everyone there gets married way before then, right?

Chick Flick Lie #17: Leave em' at the altar: No problem.

Okay, so I'm aware there are both men and women out there who have been dumped at the altar in real life. This harsh breakup doesn't just happen in the movies. However, Hollywood love stories make the wedding day dump appear to be so easy and so acceptable for everyone involved. In real life, it'd be one ugly split, and we all know it. Let's pick on the fabulous "While You Were Sleeping" once again. Lucy bails on Peter as she's walking down the aisle of forever. Let's take into account she was only marrying Peter because he wrongly believed she was his fiancé after his bout with amnesia. Still though, he was actually going to marry her. Lucy is instead in love with his brother Jack and admits it to everyone in attendance. Yeah, things get a little weird right then… In real life, Peter would probably hold a grudge toward Lucy for lying and a grudge towards Jack for stealing his fake fiancé. Oh, and as for Jack? If this were a true story, he SO wouldn't marry Lucy, due to her lying to the family about her engagement to Peter the whole time. In this dreamerville movie though? Jack proposes to Lucy, while five of his family members watch in admiration. Peter isn't present, but the tone of the movie suggests that he's all good with his brother stealing his girl.

What about the classic "Runaway Bride?" Maggie Carpenter (Julia Roberts) knows how to hook em' and how to hurt em.' Ike Graham (Richard Gere) is more than aware of her track record, but he falls victim to her charm. Though she has previously abandoned multiple men at the altar, Graham proposes to her. On the day of their wedding, she freaks out on her way to joining him in commitment. She escapes the church through a window, and hitches a ride on a FedEx truck. At the end of the flick, Maggie surrenders her running shoes and proposes to Ike…who accepts.

Then there's Serendipity, which someone I know (*cough cough*) has watched approximately 20 times. Jonathan Trager (John Cusack) and Sara Thomas (Kate Beckinsale) are both engaged to other people – yet they both remain wrapped up in a fantasy that they will one day be together. Years go by and pages turn, but they just never let go of their far-fetched hopes. John and Sara both call off their weddings without the other knowing. In the end, they run into each other on the skating rink. It was serendipity, folks…pure serendipity…Nah, I think its great scriptwriters actually.

I'm not done messing with "The Wedding Planner" either. In fact, this painfully unrealistic gem just may be the ultimate representation of this particular chick flick lie. Steve and his fiancé Fran mutually decide to call off their wedding…the day of their wedding. Both parties are happy, and they each go their separate way. Predictably, "Steve's way," includes racing to Mary and Mossimo's wedding. Ultimately, both weddings are called off, and in the end, Mary and Steve end up together. Then the credits roll…

What are these movies telling us? Leave em at the altar and everything will be just fine! No one is going to be angry about all the wasted money, all the wasted food and all the wasted time. Do this in real life? You'll definitely lose half of your Facebook friend's list and rest assured you will be removed from people's Christmas card lists. Oh, and your fiancé is especially probably not going to be saying, "Hey it's okay girl! Leave me standing here! I just want you to be happy! Go marry who you actually love…"

Chick Flick Lie #18: Girl before career.

Another one of my self-admitted favorite endings is when the man gives up his big promotion in another state - his acting or singing career or what have you…all in the name of love. A recent flick which presents this lie to the fullest is "New Years Eve." Superstar musician Jensen (Jon Bon Jovi) cancels his tour all in an attempt to win back his former fiancé Laura (Katherine Heigl). Of course she takes him back, and they toss his massive career down the drain. It really is sweet though, y'all!

In other big screen hits, the story often goes something like this: The girl cries her eyes out because the guy gets an offer to move 2,000 miles away for his new career which will consist of a six figure sum. At first he accepts, she believes they're doomed, and she writes him off. Some background music plays, and in the next few scenes, we see boxes being packed, and old pictures being looked back on, but what's he do?

Well sometimes he actually gets on the plane and leaves, but not to worry…he'll be back at her door in the next scene.

She'll say, "What are you doing here?"…and he'll say, "I turned down the job."

Or sometimes, he just plain never goes in the first place, and she says, "Aren't you supposed to be in "said" state to be the starting pitcher for "said" team?"

Then he says something like, "No baby…life with you is enough… you're all I need," or something mushy gushy like that. It's all so cute, so sweet and so dreamy, but how often does it happen in real life? Not very. In real life, Mr. Studley usually is on that airplane faster than you can say "Delta" and signing that contract faster than you can say "John Hancock." This isn't to say he doesn't occasionally think of the girl he let go, while having his calamari and champagne with the big wigs, but will he give it all up for her? Not likely. Sorry. Money and status talks.

Chick Flick Lie #19: Rain is romantic.

The famous kiss in the rain was one of my most difficult to overcome Hollywood fantasies. Rain can either be the most beautiful thing or the most annoying thing. For the typical single girl, it is probably most often annoying…unless of course, she is at home and curled up in bed. It can be relaxing to listen to the rain…don't get me wrong. For me though, whenever I have to go out into it, I associate it with being an extra struggle added to my day. It makes the morning traffic move slower, and causes me to need a massive coffee just to function for the work day. I have bad luck with umbrellas, okay? In a gust of wind, they like to flip inside out and then spill all the rain on me. I tend to get even more drenched then I would if I had just gone umbrella-less to begin with!

Apparently though, kissing in the rain is one of the most amazing feelings in the world…according to chick flicks. If the ending isn't a PDA kind of ending, we just know that they're going to reunite in the rain. That slow motion run may also be present in this conclusion. Either way, rain in a movie is almost always a romantic thing. Think of Noah and Allie in "The Notebook."

Remember the famous line, "It wasn't over for me. It still isn't over."

Then yeahhhhh…we all know what happens next.

Random sidenote: Anyone out there still distraught about Rachael McAdams and Ryan Gosling's off-screen relationship not making it the long haul? I may or may not still be completely devastated over their breakup. If Noah and Allie can't make it in real life, then who can?

Anyways, back to rain and back to the debunking of it. The real truth of rain is more like you're five miles from home on your nightly jog and that mascara you put on earlier is now running down your cheeks. Prince charming is nowhere in sight to pick you up and haul you home. However, a complete creeper does yell at you from the window of his '89 caravan, and he looks old enough to be your dad.

In a box office smash though, your makeup would still be perfect and Mr. Right would come running down the sidewalk where you'd share a kiss in the rain. Then the credits would roll and women everywhere would deem it as one of the best films of all time. I personally haven't had a romantic moment in the rain just yet (at least not that I can remember of), but I've ruined some shoes. I've ran through some puddles and wound up looking like a rat. I don't know about you though?

Chick Flick Lie #20: You always get what you want.

Plain and simple....the bottom line here is, chick flicks were founded on the idea that you always get what you want, (except for the rare occasions when someone dies, but even at that, the couple usually spends his or her final days together). Setting aside the rare exception and focusing on the typical happy-filled endings that take place in 99% of the flicks, the character ends up with exactly who they wanted. We are sold the idea that love conquers all – every obstacle, every betrayal, every issue and every difference. In the end, it comes down to "I love you and you love me." Weddings between the wrong people are easily objected, departing flights are easily stopped, and apologies are always accepted – resulting in another chance. From the "You had me at hello… you complete me" lines to the "I'm just a girl standing in front of a boy asking him to love her," statements, we continually see cheerful results.

Chick flick scripts give characters what they want, and in turn, they give viewers what they want, resulting in happy tears. However, when real life doesn't give viewers what they want, it results in sad tears instead. See how this works?

THE HARSH REALITIES OF LEAH GARDOWSKI

Guess what, friends? Now, it's time to enter the world of harsh reality. Now, it's time to see what *really* happens apart from the silver screen. As I revealed earlier, the journey of this book includes stepping into the glass slippers (more like dirty sneakers) of unsuccessful dater, Leah Gardowski.

For EVERY chick flick lie which Leah personally believed, she wound up suffering two harsh realities. She becomes pretty certain she's the victim of a love curse. Leah's life seems to be the direct opposite of chick flicks. Everything from her love life to her career is a daily fight. She's the kind of girl who waits on her knight in shining armor, but continues to get a jerk in tin foil instead.

She couldn't be more imperfect, nor could she be more real. She has big dreams which haven't quite panned out just yet. She doesn't work out every single day of her life. Sometimes life gets in the way. She shamelessly eats McDonald's dollar board more than she probably should, trips over her own feet, can't keep a white shirt clean, gets up ten minutes before she has to leave, and applies her makeup in five minutes…if she wears any at all. Life doesn't allow her to curl her hair every day, so she often sports a messy

bun. She lives average, and she's in debt. Despite the hard hits and the reoccurring disappointments, she knows how to laugh, and she knows how to live. She's universal…and for section two, she's you.

(YOU my friend, are now officially in the shoes of Leah for ALLLLLL of section two. Yes, you. Make sure you have some Xanax close by. Welcome to today's *real* dating world, folks…let the true debunking of chick flicks begin).

Harsh Leah Reality #1: The High School Sweetheart that Got Away (Thank God!)

If you are anything like Ms. Leah Gardowski, ten years later, you are likely to find you and your old flame's senior prom picture in a random box collecting dust. It may be your "ex- box," and I'm not talking about the game system here. I'm talking about that box that you stuff full with all your memorabilia from your failed relationships. You're not quite ready to throw away the pictures, the dinner receipts, the movie ticket stubs, or those dried, but long dead roses he gave you for a long ago Valentine's Day just yet. Soooo…you create a box in which you can store these tidbits of your past - yet not look at them every day.

In that box, you find your senior prom couple picture in a generic, tarnished frame that says, "Dance the Night Away," (and you think to yourself, "What a pathetically lame, but once beautiful at the time theme.") Gosh, why did you spend $200 on that hideous out of style gown? You guess it was in style then…but HOW!? It took a lot of getting chewed out by "mad at the world customers" to afford that poofy thing. It'd sure be nice to have that large chunk of change back! Not to mention, the meanest girl in the school wore the same exact one that evening. Everyone kept commenting about how cute it was that you two dressed alike, as if she sent you some sort of a memo, and you graciously accepted her Bobbsey twin's invitation. By the end of the night, you would've been happier to have worn one of those puke green tablecloths, which apparently was one of your classes' chosen colors. Ohhhh…and your hair?! Did you go to an actual stylist, or did you just simply stick your finger in the nearest light socket? Your self-applied makeup job? Let's not even go there…you don't need any nightmares tonight.

Your Prince Charming of the evening you either:

A. Hardly remember
B. Parted ways with before college
C. Is married to one of your so-called "friends,"
D. Perhaps already divorced from that Caribbean gal that he left you for on your senior class trip. Two wives, two kids and 50 pounds of excess weight later, he sure isn't the prince charming you remember.

That's when you start dwelling on and thinking about the Garth Brooks song entitled, "Unanswered Prayers." You just know that this smash hit was written just for YOU! Sadly, your high school story isn't "The Breakfast Club" or "Sixteen Candles" where high school love conquers all in the end. Your story is also a far cry from "Drive Me Crazy," as Nicole's prom date wound up being quite the success – unlike yours. As the credits rolled, you were CERTAIN these couples would grow old and gray together, and in Hollywood terms, they did. You were also certain that in real life your high school love would be sitting next to you in a luxurious retirement home one day, but you were wrong. So wrong!

So now it's apparent that you didn't marry your high school sweetheart, and you still are in need of Mr. Right to complete your "Unanswered Prayers" story. Relax sister! Not all fairy tales are for the high school aged! There's plenty of, if not more movies, in which Mr. Right comes along in later adulthood. In fact, most Disney princesses appear to be in their mid 20's, or at least close to it! Again, relax sister! It isn't too late for you! Don't worry about your current circumstances. No true beauty will ever, I mean EVER, be heartbroken drowning in a bed of tears with her Ben & Jerry's (the only two men who will always comfort her in her time of need). No true beauty will ever be the picture of this miserable fictional character once she reaches the age of 25. Nope, that wasn't EVER going to happen to you. You had your five year plan all written in stone, and your ten year plan in progress and pending certification. Right? Wrong!

Harsh Leah Reality #2: The College Sweetheart that Got Away (Once Again, Thank God!)

So fast forward to age 25…your college sweetheart who you were nearly engaged to, cheated on you a week after you earned your Master's degree. No biggie! Suck it up, slip on some sweatpants and a big sweatshirt, take a drive, run by the nearest Sonic or DQ, get you some ice cream to go, pop in a funny movie, curl up with your puppy in a blanket…and then, let that undeserving, poor excuse for a man, go! Who wants to be tied down by 25 anyways? C'mon now…25 is the new 16…at least that's what you've been hearing these days!

The problem is - this breakup IS a BIGGIE to you, despite your friend's words of encouragement and pleas to let the loser go. Still, you love that loser, and you are crushed over his unfaithfulness towards you. You now consider your high school love to be a horrific imitation of real love. THIS was real love. You were really hoping for an Elle Woods' "Legally Blonde" kind of story. You were supposed to graduate college with honors, an offer for your dream job and a man…THIS man to be exact. Despite the fact that Dillon skipped most of his undergraduate classes (before dropping out) to play video games, had a dorm room so messy you couldn't see the floor, had old food sticking to his dishes, and got fired from his video game job (the only job you still know of him to have had till this day), you really saw promise in this guy. True promise. You were willing to let him have his man cave, and you were willing to be the breadwinner of the household. At least back then you were. Moving right along..

Harsh Leah Reality #3: There's one in Every Workplace

Okay, so now it's time to turn the page and embark on the next chapter in your life. You're in your first professional job, which consists of your own desk, a personalized name plate, ID badge, and you're big stuff. You can't help but notice your new cubicle neighbor. He's got eyes that pierce the heart and a smile that brings sunshine on a cloudy day! His left hand appears to be naked of any life-long covenant. He doesn't have any pictures of anyone in his workspace, which leads you to believe there isn't any wife or children involved. You thought maybe at first you were imagining things, but it appears that you're not…he's flirting with you! Alas, your long awaited fairy tale is finally coming true, and "happily ever after congratulations" are in order! C'mon now, most of the greatest "chick flicks" do start in the work place, and you my dear, will be no exception. You've seen this work out so well in the movies. Both "The Proposal" and "Confessions of a Shopaholic" have given you such hope in workplace relationships!

It won't be long before you're standing in front of the preacher saying your "I do's," and naming your children. Nothing worked out before because you were meant to wait for this moment, and now that it's finally here……………you find out in a random conversation over donuts and orange juice with Lucinda (the office know it all), that Mr. Right is "married," and doesn't want you to know! Ugh, what a conniving pig! You always knew the truth deep down. Why did you shut your intuition up? You always knew he was too good to be true! Who in their right mind would want a work relationship anyways? Who wants to take their work home with them at night? So long, you lying pig! You may be out to cheat on your wife, but it certainly won't be with me!

Harsh Leah Reality #4: Men Who Play Guitar Also Play Hearts

Go on and treat yourself to a night out. Take the tags off that cute dress, try out that liquid eyeliner, and throw on those fabulous stilettos that you have finally learned how to walk in. Catch you some good live music and good times with the girls! Isn't single life great? You're feeling so free, so alive, so on top of the world, and so, so…LOVE-STRUCK by the lead singer who is clearly making eyes at you! Alas, the ideal fairy tale! Every little girl dreams of marrying a rock star! Sure he currently smokes enough pot to fill his entire tour bus and drinks enough whiskey to fill a distillery, but he is into you, and he will change! Just be supportive, understanding, and meet him right where he's at. In the movies these types of men always change their ways for the one they love. Right? In the movies, yes…but this is real life here.

Okay, so fast forward to six months later…the guitar serenades and the 3 a.m. talks have come to an abrupt halt. Mr. Rock Star has exited the picture, not because you wanted him to, but simply because you do not even know where he is. Heck, he probably doesn't even know where he is. After threatening, yet definitely resisting to take up pot and binge drinking yourself, just to ease the pain as a not-so-positive coping method, you finally decide your true winner is yet to be found. "Thing Called Love" caused you to believe you would marry a musician someday. How were you to know that in real life, so many of these men have ongoing commitment issues? Yeah, you never hear from him again…ever. This rock and roller is about as gentle with hearts as he is on his guitar. Maybe you should've listened when Journey sang, "Loving a music man ain't always what it's supposed to be"…and then NOT listened when they go on to say, "I'm forever yours…faithfully." Oh, and don't listen when they say "Don't Stop Believing" either.

Harsh Leah Reality #5: The Boy Next Door

After a bit of a dating hiatus, you are beautifully interrupted by a new job…AND a new man at your brand spanking new apartment complex. Yes, you've lived in apartment complexes before, and you were simply not attracted to "Mr. Too into You" at your last one, but this place of residence is in a league of its own. The scenery of this place is beautiful in more ways than one, and you're not just talking about their landscaping work. You are finally realizing what it is like to live in the lap of luxury. You are finally experiencing some of the fun you were never able to have in college. In fact, this place is beginning to put you in mind of a college campus...but these guys actually have jobs. Young, good-looking, single guys are simply crawling the place, and to top it all off, you know that you are being "checked out" by several of them. You might be oblivious at times...but not THAT oblivious.

In the midst of being checked out and becoming fairly certain that you are America's latest 'Bachelorette,' you are especially intrigued by one particular neighbor...your next door neighbor to be exact. Yep, that's right! You don't give any matter to the fact that his bedroom wall is your living room wall, and that you cannot escape the premises without walking past his door (unless you choose to take a superhero sort of leap from the third story). Never mind, he would then watch you plummet to your embarrassing injuries from his window...sooooo that wouldn't be worth it. Seriously though, if you two were to start something only to crash and burn, your new princess loft could soon feel more like a dungeon. (Think "Beauty and the Beast" style). You also don't give any matter to warnings your friends give you...because he is the one!

You knew he was going to be your last love from the day you met outside his door. You had NO idea whatsoever that you had such an adorable neighbor until that moment. If you had known that you were going to run into Matt Damon's lookalike that day, you certainly wouldn't have literally just rolled out of bed, threw on the oldest, ugliest clothing you have, left the place with messy hair, and not even a hint of makeup on. To top it all off, you're carrying your trash bag. So yeah, you pretty much look like the garbage lady to put it mildly. Oddly though, 'Mr. Next Door,' says hello, and gives you that "I'm into you" grin. Between his sparkling blue eyes and his smile which makes you believe he is a toothpaste model, you are seriously smitten by Mr. 1332 at first sight. For the first time in months – you Ms. 1331, flash a real smile...not one of those fake ones which you had gotten so good at.

Amazingly, he offers to take your trash for you. Surely he just feels sorry for you!...because uhhhhh, look at you! After you politely decline and allow your bold independence to get the best of you, you put that smelly bag of trash into your car, knowing full well that it is probably going to leak into your back seat. That perfect looking man was just going to throw it on his truck bed, which would have made much more sense.

Well thankfully for you, your stubbornness didn't turn him off too much. After a few more smile and giggle encounters, it was clear he wasn't going to be *just* the "boy next door" to you. You started telling your friends cheesy things like, "This guy has put the light back in my eyes again"...and even cheesier, "The fact that he gave me such butterflies makes me realize I can actually feel all fluttery again. I didn't know that was possible, girls."

Every time you spoke with him, your confidence increased. One night out by his truck, you finally learn he has an actual name other than "Boy Next Door." You even learned about his job and his recent college graduation. The quick connection was clear, and you were laughing and smiling like you had known each other for a good while. You still couldn't get over his wide welcoming smile, and you knew right then and there, you could happily get real used to it. As he talked, his ocean blue eyes seemed to smile right along with him. He informed you that the click-clack of your high heels walking by in the morning is what let him know it was time for him to leave for work also. Finally he told you to come by anytime. His invitation caused you to smile another authentic smile.

"Walking on Sunshine" had become your theme song. Your best friend was excited to see you full of life again. She convinced you to ask him out to the sporting event which you had just won tickets to. Though you were incredibly hesitant about being the pursuer, you felt like he may actually be the type to like it. Could the former shyest girl in her whole entire school actually do something like this?

You can still remember getting ready to knock on his door with those sweaty palms. A small part of you realized he may have a girlfriend, or he may just in fact be a really friendly person with zero romantic interest in you. Then came the knock and then came the opening of the door. Though he seemed glad to see you, he didn't open the door all the way or invite you in, because frankly, it was a huge mess in there. It just reaffirmed to you that he was real..

After date one, you were pretty much inseparable for the next few months. Your chemistry was off the charts and nothing prior to this had ever felt so natural. Every morning before work, you would swing by for a big hug and kiss before going on your way. He usually knew to open the door just by the sound of the high heels coming, and he officially gave you the nickname "Click-Clack." He later admitted to purposely running into you on several occasions prior to truly knowing you, and checking you out through the peephole a time or two…and you weren't even creeped out. Not even remotely. Staying in for TV and cuddle time was all you needed when you were with him. You were the most relaxed you had been in years. You goofed off, you swapped stories, and you laughed. You also used to text and check on each other to make sure one another got home alright with it being such a long walk and all. It was the closest experience to a chick flick you've ever had. It was close…but no cigar – and maybe that's the most painful kind of story in existence.

From the get-go, your relationship with this guy bared a strong resemblance to the classic story of Paul Varjak and Holly Golightly… except, you never did have "Breakfast at Tiffany's." Still, it sounded so cute to say you were literally seeing the boy next door. When Mr. 1332 moved across town, things fell apart, but would they stay apart?

Shortly after your latest blow, Jarrett the boy downstairs came up, knocked on your door, and asked you out on a date. Maybe "Boy Downstairs" just didn't have the same ring to it, but you remained stuck on "Boy Next Door"…Consequently, after a date with Jarrett, you quickly let him know you weren't ready for anything..

So after some time passes…you realize that you've dated from the same apartment complex building twice, and it's boldly obvious that you should probably start dating elsewhere. "Should" is the key word here. There are simply too many attractive prospects here to stop and rest on your laurels. You have officially given new meaning to the term "speed dating." If you don't like one guy you go out on a date with, the solution is easy: Go for his neighbor instead. Every time a new guy moves in to your complex, you're about as excited as a kid on Christmas morning. Ahhh…complex dating is your new enticement, and the effortlessness of it all fits so perfectly with your laziness.

However, as a wannabe Miss Golightly, you remain stuck on the fantasy of your wannabe Mr. Varjak…for years. Though it's a Rocky Road (not the kind of Rocky Road you enjoy indulging in), the plot continues, and he remains a staple in your life. The only harsh reality in this scenario is that the world's cutest story doesn't seem like it's going to get the perfect happy ending. Still, the two of you remain a loose end as two friends who aren't really just friends. He's the one who never ends, and you like it that way…no matter how dysfunctional it may be. If the story doesn't end well when it's all said and done…you really don't want to know right now…

Harsh Leah Reality #6: The Boy Back Home

Though Boy Next Door made you melt a bit, and maybe made you lose your edge and your consistent sarcasm just a bit…you are still you, right? You will pick yourself up from this (maybe). Just to spice up life, the boy back home who you have always liked suddenly returns to your life. It never did go beyond a friendship, but it sure always had the potential to be one of the greatest love stories of all times. Yes! This is the best kind of chick flick..the kind that goes it's separate ways after high school, but always ends up right back to where it's supposed to be. It is the classic bad timing then, good timing now, story. It's kind of like "Hope Floats" without the ugly divorce.

Before you know it, you two are texting every single day, and you're even planning a trip to the home front, just knowing you will soon be "official." After all, he admitted to having such a crush on you for the past 20-something years, and he continually reminds you how happy he is to have you in his life. He even goes as far to say that he always wanted you to be the one. He talks all big about your future together, and you start making plans for a fun-filled year. He finally requests you as a friend on Facebook, and you're so excited to watch this love story unfold. You have that stupid smile on your face, and you have to contain yourself from bursting! Two days later, you notice that he has made some updates on his Facebook, and you're just so sure in his process of page renovation that he's put some adorable quote or tidbit about you on there. The incredibly cheesy expression on your face remains as you look through his adorable page.

Your eyes then land on his relationship status…and you notice that he is now in a relationship, which would be great if it was YOUR name listed after the word "with." Ahem, your much deserved name is NOT in that spot! You always knew that the sneaky Suzanna Blackburn was out to steal your man! It's okay though, sister…it really is! Who needs a guy from the past anyways? You don't want such a large taste of home to impede your personal growth anyways! While you're strutting down the red carpet in your sequin gown and picking up yet another award, she will be screaming in that horrible looking hospital gown and popping out yet another kid. Not that there's anything wrong with that, but what would YOU rather be doing at THAT moment? Get over your wanna-be "Sweet Home Alabama" story, and move on sister!

Still, even with your excessive daydreams, you are beyond bummed about this latest kick in the face. You treat yourself to a pedicure and a shopping spree. Then you proceed to tell yourself, "This too shall pass." Yes, that's all you get done telling yourself…but "it" always does pass… and "it" of course moves on to something even more drama-filled. "It" just gets a little worse, right?

Harsh Leah Reality #7: Business or Pleasure?

Six months and six billion tears later, you are finally feeling good again! You're a year older, but age is only a number…at least, that's what Mama keeps telling you! Bless her heart! She always tries her hardest to keep you from coming to grips with the harsh realities taking place in your loco life. Nonetheless, it's okay that you're older, because apparently you were meant to meet Mr. Right on your business trip to Florida at this very age. The timing is perfect…just perfect! Now that you are getting some of your college debts paid off, you are ready to take the plunge, tie the knot, and fill up the house of your dreams with love and babies. You wouldn't have been ready for this big step years ago! However, now, you're ready to drive that SUV, buy everything on those infomercials, read bedtime stories, and wear holiday sweaters (okay you're NEVER doing that one), but you're ready to "mom it up." It's also true that the best chick flicks often entail long distance stories. As the classic saying goes, "distance makes the heart grow fonder."

Your dreamy "Mr. Not a Moment Too Soon" man flies in for a visit. He's got roses, a card, and a magic kiss on the lips, waiting just for you. The weekend is going so great! Heck, you wouldn't be surprised if he proposes tonight. After all, he's brought up marriage with you on more than one occasion recently. Why would either of you want to be apart much longer anyways? Distance has been a good challenge that has definitely made the two of you stronger, but now love must be together. He says he has something very important to tell you, and you just know what's coming next…but where will the wedding be?! Shall you say your vows here, in Florida on the beach, or somewhere in between?!

You're fantasizing about your big day and all of the fine details – the flowers, the cake, the colors, and the centerpieces, when suddenly you hear the four words…but not the four words you expected. Could he have mistakenly said "I need a break," instead of the "Will you marry me," that you were expecting? You guess you must have heard him right the first time, because he's got a one-way ticket…HOME! For some screwed up reason that you yourself cannot even comprehend, you are even nice enough to drive him to the airport for his departure out of your life. Never in your recollection have you worked so hard to hold tears back. Your "I'm just fine & I totally agree with the breakup" façade is wearing real thin…real fast.

As you say your good-byes, you feel like you're dying inside. Of course he wrongly believes he's making things better by saying the classic, "You're a great girl. Whoever ends up with you is going to be a lucky man," line. You really wish he would just move along, because the tears welling up in your eyes could probably fill an entire bucket (of fried chicken), if allowed to fall. Instead of watching him walk out of your life and waving one last good-bye, you quickly jump into your vehicle that is nearing "empty," and drive away like you're on a high speed chase.

"Distance doesn't make the heart grow fonder!" Sadly, you fell for yet another Hollywood lie! "Out of sight, out of mind" is more like it. You think of all the "whys," "what ifs," and "might've beens," as you continue to drive through the tears with the radio on full blast. You can barely even see the road your whole miserable fifteen minute drive, which feels like forever today. Every song on the radio makes you want to chop your hair off and wear black nail polish, no matter what station you flip it to. You finally arrive home, and run into your poor excuse for an apartment as if your butt is on fire. Then of course, you collapse onto your bed sobbing, making your white pillow case black with mascara.

Despite the river of tears, you assure yourself that "this isn't over yet." No, in every great chick flick, the man realizes his mistake and runs off that plane as fast as he can. Also, you distinctly remember him saying "I need a break." "I need a break" is quite different from "I want to break up." "I need a break" implies that he will be back. Maybe all he needed was a five minute break! Yes, it's only a matter of time before Romeo jumps out of that plane, grabs a taxi as fast as he can, and kneels at your door step begging for you to take him back. He will be singing you a song that he wrote on his way there, with the guitar a fellow flyer gave him. It will be kind of like "How to Lose a Guy in 10 Days" meets "The Wedding Singer." It will be perfect...just perfect. While his performance may be terribly off key, it will be the most beautiful sound you've ever heard. He will be back...you just know it!......or perhaps, you'll never see him again...ever! You knew he was still in love with his "ex." Your "he's got someone else on his mind" radar went off a long time ago! Six months later he pops the big question...to her.

Harsh Leah Reality #8: Granny plays wing woman

You will be okay…yes, you most certainly will! The sweet elderly lady at your Tuesday night Bingo club has insisted upon you meeting her grandson. (Bingo isn't just for seniors anymore. In fact, it is actually quite fun and great for stress relief. Got it? Good!) Soooo…now you have a new prospect that is reportedly intelligent, caring, and almost done with med school. Just your new adopted Grandma's description alone makes you want to call out "Bingo!" She didn't have to scheme and fake a choking attack like the granny in "Hitch," but she was pretty smooth in the way in which she introduced the two of you.

You meet this intriguing possibility one dark night out by his souped-up sports car that he is picking her up in. Clearly, you wouldn't have to worry about the future if you had a guy like him around. From what you can tell, he just may be exactly what you've been looking for. Then again, that pathological lying "this could be it" thought has been replaying in your mind like a broken record for the past ten years. (Just for the record, YOU have broken this record, because you're sick of it and the stupid songs it plays over and over again).

Nonetheless, you brush aside your negative pessimism and get in touch with your positive perspective of things. Yes, this perspective still exists…but just barely. The light at the end of the tunnel isn't exactly a life-sized chandelier anymore, but it is at least close to being a night light. This studious grandson seems a little shy, but his match-making Grandma coaxes him into asking you out on Friday night. Since you're not an idiot (well, that's debatable)…you still know better than to turn down such a catch…even though you are still wounded from "Mr. Florida" and of course "Boy Next Door."

You decide to be optimistic and wear that perfect classy, yet sexy dress that you've been saving for just the right occasion. You don't spend four hours getting ready for dates like you once did…an hour has become your new rule. Why set aside one-sixth of your precious day for someone who might turn out to be the loser of the decade? Also, if he doesn't like the natural you…he sure isn't going to like you in a month when you start sporting the messy bun and make-up free face, after you push yourself too hard in the gym. Okay…back to the date!

He picks you up in the same souped-up sports car that you saw the other night, and you have a great conversation all the way to the upscale restaurant he is taking you to for dinner. It's been a long time since a man has treated you to anywhere even remotely close to this. You are finally seeing him in the light for the first time, and while you don't want to gawk at him, he looks fairly cute.

Upon your server's enthusiastic second welcome, you decide to order a cup of soup because:

A. You don't want him to think that you are a pig,
B. It seems easy enough to eat,
C. In case of the crazy unforeseen event that you end up paying, you can't afford the sirloin platter with only $6 to your name.

Ohhh and D. You want something that you can scarf down quickly in case this date becomes an utter nightmare. It's happened before and you know it could happen again…but you are feeling GREAT about this man. You're just simply playing on the safe side.

"Mr. Almost Done with Med School" is polite, successful, attentive and funny…looking! He's not obnoxiously funny looking, but he has really weird teeth, and to make matters worse, sometimes he snorts when he laughs. Good call on ordering that soup, sister! The louder he snorts…the faster you eat. It's all just too much of a deal breaker, even if those other girls would think you're lucky! You just KNEW something was going to go wrong with this…especially since he was SO into you. While it's a true shame, "Mr. Almost Done with Med School" isn't the one for you! Apparently he thought you were the one for him though… and so did Granny. Since you broke his heart AND Grandma's, you drop out of your Bingo Club, and upgrade your Tuesday nights to a scrapbooking class instead.

This by far isn't the first time this kind of unfortunate situation has happened to you. Over the years, your friends have gasped as you have turned down what they believed to be perfectly suitable suitors! For just a few of the countless examples, there was of course "Mr. Too into You" at your last apartment complex that would have done anything for you, but you didn't want him to. Even if you cut the circulation off in your wrists by carrying those 30 shopping bags up three flights of stairs at once...it was well worth it to avoid his advances. Then, there was your friend Janelle's cousin Todd who was totally infatuated with you. You told him there just wasn't a connection between the two of you, but he thought you were a match made in Heaven. Oh, and of course there was that amazing "Mr. I Have it Altogether" guy that you met in your Church group. You especially still kick yourself for rejecting this dedicated man of God who was going on to seminary school - knowing he would have been an ideal husband for almost anyone. Sadly though, you know you would still do the same thing even if you had another chance with him. He was an incredible listener with great morals, but you just simply weren't attracted to him. There was no amount of convincing that anyone could do, because there was nothing you could do about your lack of attraction towards him. Unfortunately you are starting to realize that you never seem to want what is readily available to you. You only seem to want that which you cannot have. You are helplessly attracted to danger, and apparently to idiocy.

Harsh Leah Reality #9: "SHE" Gets Flowers...

Nothing is more irritating than the moment that you realize your on-again off-again boyfriend Blake buys flowers for anyone and everyone, but you. Not that you'd expect him to buy you flowers NOW, but he sure didn't then...and now, he appears to be more full of flowers than a greenhouse. Okay, he's full of something else too (something that doesn't smell anything like flowers)..but seriously, what is he now...a florist? No, he most likely didn't go through an occupation change, but the point is...he suddenly buys colorful bouquets of perfection for everyone from his co-worker who had a bad day, to of course his new gal who he has been dating a whole week…(who probably claims she has a bad day every day).

Her latest Instagram addition says, "I've got the best boyfriend in the world. #BeautifulFlowers #LuckyGirl." All you can do is sit there and think…#Annoyed, #WantToMakeASmartAleckCommentBack, #IWantADislikeButton, but instead you decide to un-follow her. Yes, another one of your so-called friends was interested in being far more than friends with the man you once called "yours."

You keep your harsh thoughts to yourself, but you're thinking:

"How come I never got any flowers in the three years I spent dating him?"

"I should have got SOMETHING for the misery that I went through!"

Suddenly, you can totally identify with Jane in "27 dresses," while she watches her wanna-be love George shower Tess with gorgeous flowers. It's all almost too much to watch. Then you realize…you never received any because you were too strong of a person…yeah, that's right. You didn't whine about your bad days, you only cried in front of him once (that dang onion was wicked), and you never acted like you needed much of anything from him. Perhaps that was your fault, but you can't help it that you're not a weakling. It's just not you by nature. It doesn't de-feminize you or take away your need for a little pampering every now and then.

Oh well, you sit back and look around your apartment…and then you remember, you DO have flowers…the fake ones, that last forever of course. They have dust on them an inch thick, but it's the best you can do for yourself. After all, you really can't keep anything alive except yourself anyways…and some days, that's even a battle. You are the only person you know that can kill a perennial flower to such a degree that it doesn't even make an attempt to return the next year.

All this thinking about flowers causes you to You Tube Jaron And The Long Road to Love's "Pray For You" song.

"I pray your brakes go out running down the hill…

I pray a flower pot falls from the window sill…
And knocks you in the head like I'd like to…
I pray your birthday comes and nobody calls…
I pray you're flying high when the engine stalls…"

Before you know it, you've hit repeat five times. You've even become a hair brush singing sensation in your living room, and you don't care who hears or sees you. Since you live on the third floor you daydream about accidently knocking off that flower pot of your dead flowers… and it accidently hitting your ex.

Sigh..every time you promise yourself that you're going to do better with your thought life and the words of your mouth, something just has to push you over the edge (like a flying flower pot, of course). Ah, you just can't get that thought out of your mind. Like Jaron, you make your way to church, and you tell yourself that your thought life is going to become more like that of Mother Teresa…but you're still quite the project.

Harsh Leah Reality #10: Pinning Your Life Away

(Note: For anyone who may have been living under a rock for the past few years, Pinterest is the website in which so many people are going to create picture boards of interest. It is ultimately where either domesticated or aspiring domesticated women find and save pictures to match up with their own Hollywood-like fantasies. Whether you are looking for the perfect outfit, silky flowing hair, DIY projects, crockpot meals, a divine cake, the dream wedding gown, or everything in between…you can find it on Pinterest).

In the very hour that you say you've sworn off men, you find yourself browsing Pinterest, and posting all your ideas for your future, currently non-existent wedding. Ahhhh…these table covers are uhhhh-mazing, and ohhh…these colors would be beyond gorgeous for an outdoor wedding. Perhaps I want to get married in a glamorous barn…

no, no,..maybe in an old southern plantation house! Well, the idea of getting married on the beach has always sounded extra romantic. Then again, you always told yourself as a little girl you would have the traditional church wedding. Hmm, well that photo from the spur of the moment chapel wedding looks super fun, and you've always been soooo spontaneous! Whatever will you decide!? Should you drink from mason jars or fancy stemmed glasses for the bride and groom toast? You thought you wanted to wear your hair down with a tiara, but that low out of the face hair-do may look even better. Oh man, now you have 1,000 ideas for your "something old," 1,001 pins for your something "borrowed," and approximately 1,002 different thoughts for your "something new and something blue." Ahhhh, and those engagement pictures are EPIC! You always thought you wanted to take yours out in a big open field with your hair blowing in the wind. However, now the black and white photos with "June 10th: Save the Date" written in sidewalk chalk beside you and your soon to be hubby is really sparking your interest.

Then you proceed to browse the food and drink section for all the recipes you plan to cook for your non-existent husband and children, and all the DIY crafts and organization tips you tell yourself you'll do later. Once you're done with all that, you jump on over to the child rearing tips, because you plan on having the most amazing children in the country. Then you pin upteen ideas on how to decorate your future elaborate dream home with the porch that wraps all the way around. Then the ADD kicks in even more. Oh goodness, you haven't checked out the David's Bridal website in a week or so, and you have GOT to prioritize that dress. You really need to put first things first! You never know what kind of out of this world gowns they may be featuring now.

While you're dreaming of your destination honeymoon and your future flawless marriage, indulging in your trusty comfort food, the reality suddenly brutally sinks in:

"Ohhh, wait…that's right, I don't have a man. I swore them off. JUST in case, I ever change my mind though…THIS is what I want! And oh yea, I better get to the gym, and allow Gabby Gabe (the pretend gym rat) to feed me his usual unappealing pickup lines for the night, while he lifts five pound dumbbell weights and grunts like he's the Hulk."

Yep, you need to close that laptop, throw away that M & M bag that you have now emptied, put on those yoga pants that you swear you're going to rip someday, and head on over. Sigh…back to reality princess!

Harsh Leah Reality #11: Radar Chips & The UFHO (Underground Female Hating Organization)

For a good while, you've numbed your heartbreak by working more than what is humanely healthy. It was as if you tuned out relationships completely for a good while, but then as soon as you became open to love again, you were bombarded. You've had way too many dates in the past few years, and some really pathetic relationships in between. You know you're self-sufficient and you know you don't *need* a man – but you do miss having one. You have FINALLY decided to either move on to a new guy, or maybe even to just recycle one of your old ones yet again. Yes, that's right.

"Recycle, renew, reuse"…makes you think of a song you used to sing off television as a child.

Between the fact that Mama taught you to recycle, and the fact that you were raised a church girl having Christ-like patience for nearly everyone, no matter how many times they disappoint you, you are usually pretty easily lured back in, and all your exes know it. For some reason, *none* of your exes, except the married ones, ever leave you alone. You say you're done forever, but sweet words have always been your weakness. Whenever one casts his line, you are guilty of going right for the bait without much hesitation. Maybe he's going to change this time, right? Maybe he's been the one this WHOLE time. Granted he's the master of disappointment, but maybe not today! They all talk about the sunshine you bring to their lives, which is an interesting concept, because for you, they are beginning to feel like a reoccurring storm that just rages on and on, because they always end up gone and gone…

Understandably, you're always about as confused as Paris Hilton would be in an Advanced Calculus class.

Though you have several reoccurring dysfunctional relationships, "Blake" has always been your main go-to. Yes, Blake, as in the guy who never buys you flowers, but apparently does so for every other woman friend – but anyways, he's newly single again. You first met him shortly after your college graduation. You were friends first, then you were more than friends, then you were not friends, then you were full-fledged dating again, then you were confused, then you were friends again…Okay, something like that. This guy just can't get it right… period. However, there is always this small part of you that likes lying to yourself, believing that he is the one in the end. Sadly, you may even love that old familiar misery you feel when he's taking you on the dangerous ride of confusion. He's been taking you down the same road for years, yet you refuse to get off the train. So there you are watching life just pass you by, all new scenery is a blur, and every now and then this train just wrecks. When it wrecks for the 25th time, you think you and him are officially done. You swear you are. That is until he returns…again. When does he typically return? The second you swear you're over him, have happily rediscovered your independence, or of course when you have begun either talking to someone new, or of course when you are reuniting with yet another old ex that can't get it right.

The weirdest thing about Blake? Somehow he always knows the most opportune time to contact you. He must have a radar chip that goes off, because you know that he actually has no way of really knowing you're moving on otherwise. You are always extremely private and vague on your Facebook and Twitter accounts, and since your off and on like a light switch relationship has been pretty much a secret for the past seven years, there aren't really any mutual friends that could tell him what's going on, and if you even have mutual friends, most of them probably don't even know about your relationship…or whatever it is. Besides, Blake so isn't a "Facebooker."

Seriously, the only thing that can explain his "knowing he needs to pop up," is that he has some kind of new radar technology chip that has been implanted into his brain.

It says something like, "Houston! We have a problem! She is starting to get over you, and may be considering someone new! Make sure to go sabotage it, smooth talk her, keep her hanging on, and restore some of that false hope she has in you. Then, be sure to run away again, and stay away until I alert you again next time. In the meantime, I'm going to alert her other ex-jerk to go play with her head once again. Over and out..."

The craziest part of all is that whatever guy you begin warming up to again - will suddenly walk away yet again. Rest assured though, he will return later with a whole new game plan. You may ignore his texts and calls for a good while, but he always finds a way to come through, and a way to make you believe that everything will be different this time. It's always the wrong guy popping up at the wrong time. Apparently they ALL have this mysterious radar chip implant. You imagine there is some secret coalition or meeting place where all these guys meet up and are in cahoots with one another.

Then who returns? Alex. The other one you recently swore off after a bad third date. You know the story that continually repeats itself: You start slowly warming up to Alex who seems to have it altogether for a week or two. Then he proceeds to become cooler than a cucumber and disappears into thin air. That's okay though...you're not really feeling him anyways...at all. Maybe he caught onto that? He should probably move along...

Once Alex leaves the picture again, guess who presses your buttons by texting the world's sweetest text message? Ex-boyfriend, Corey! Wow, you thought you and him were done when you told him off last year for his excessively flirty ways, but everyone deserves a second chance, right? Wrong. You give him that second chance, and then he decides to go off with some other girl...or at least you think? It's not like he gave you an explanation for his disappearance. That would just be too dang considerate of him right!? Right.

Then guess who's back again? Blake! Sure, he's been gone for two months, and you've re-tried Alex and Corey both in between, but you decide to give Blake his 26th chance. For a good two weeks this time (which may in fact be a record), Blake seems to be living up to his smooth words. The second you start falling for it? You guessed it. He's gone again.

The second he's gone? "Beep, beep," says Corey's head!

"Text Leah immediately!!"

Of course in the midst of everything, cheaters from your past decide to return. College boyfriend Dillon randomly calls you to pour out his heart. You wish you could find a nice sugar-coated way to tell him that he has a better chance of winning the $300 million dollar Powerball than he does of ever getting you back. However, you don't do sugar-coating and you can't find a nice way…so you tell him exactly what's on your mind. You're pretty sure you made him cry, but you assure yourself that as long as he has his video games, he'll be fine.

Then up pops Joe Limburtony – the ultimate cheater who truly believes he's God's gift to women. His words are smoother than silk, and his good looks are hard to resist, but your six month post-college relationship with him was one big lie. Since you don't allow men to disrespect you, he has even less of a chance than Dillon has of ever winning you back…and that's pretty bad. (Read on to find out how truly despicable this Joe character really is).

If that isn't enough, there's this new guy Carter that has just begun texting you. Leave it to Blake to mysteriously text you on your first date with Carter telling you he misses you more than you know. For a good three weeks, you are ignoring texts from all of your exes, and you start to believe that Carter could in fact be hubby material…until he joins the others on their never-ending quest of confusing you. You don't need to mess with these commitment-shy men though. No…you have turned down several good guys these past few months, because you just don't feel it. Of course you don't. Anything good for you = you not being interested, right? You are officially angry with yourself, but don't know how to make yourself want someone – nor do you want to find out.

Yep, you are pretty sure these not so worthy men have a secret club where they meet and map out a plan of who is going to do what and when. Maybe some local restaurant has some kind of secret room, or your city has some "Underground Female Hating Organization" (UFHO) that you're unaware about. You still are highly speculating that it could be that new technological radar chip in the brain as well. Either that or you're on that "Punk'd" or "Candid Camera," show and Ashton Kutcher or some host is fixing to reveal to you that everything has been a joke thus far. Maybe there is a new secret reality show on television that you didn't agree to be the star of…or maybe, you have yet to awake from a crazy dream? Perhaps these guys are all reading the same best-selling book of strategies you haven't yet heard about. Whatever the reason, timing is NOT your friend, and you're evidently not supposed to be married yet, but you are beyond tired of this exhausting ride that never seems to end. Maybe you should pick up a third job to keep your mind occupied? You should probably change your phone number too..

Harsh Leah Reality #12: Therapy (When Bubble Wrap is No Longer Enough)

After all the crazy UFHO/radar chip/reality TV/crazy dream events of lately, you decide to begin therapy. Yes, that's right. The first step in solving a problem is admitting that you have one. You majored in counseling yourself, though you never used your degree. Well, you've never been paid to use it at least. You have been the town counselor since you moved here, and you love every minute of helping others, but you question if your advice can possibly be sound advice. Counselors aren't supposed to be train wrecks. Therefore, this is one of those times when the counselor needs a counselor. You have officially popped each bubble of the bubble wrap from your latest purchase of self-help books. The book's advice proved worthless and the bubble wrap was only a temporary high.

You know the stereotypes which go with seeing a counselor all too well. However, you decide you may benefit from one as you do believe in what they do. You are convinced you are a deeper thinker than Einstein though (at least when it comes to relationships and useless life stuff), and you are pretty sure no one can get through your thick skull...not even a paid professional. You go into therapy with your head held high and your expectations for release of confusion even higher. At this point, your options are few.

Session one goes pretty well, though you find yourself knowing most of what he is going to say before he says it.

"How does that make you feel?" he asks.

"Pretty dang crappy and confused," you respond.

"What are your options in the matter?," he asks.

"Umm...I guess to either allow myself to stay confused, or to let go of all of them and start over."

"Right," he answers, and "stop over-thinking things. Just enjoy life, and let it be what it's going to be."

Though you KNEW what he was going to say, the venting felt okay, and it was also good to have confirmation that you're not "crazy." However, he may think that you ARE crazy, but isn't saying anything about it because you're a lost cause, and he doesn't want to make a crazy person crazier by telling them the truth about themselves? Perhaps! You are also kind of getting tired of him insinuating that you just take your adversities and "suck it up," when you know he himself is the classic happily married father of three. How can this man possibly understand YOU? He obviously doesn't want to be alone in life either...

Still though, it was kind of good to know that you were talking to someone who is paid to listen and has thoroughly studied people. The sad part of all of it though is that you have sooooo many guys and details going, that your counselor can't keep them straight. You spend nearly a whole session just explaining who each guy is, where he comes from, and his story to the point where your situation never actually gets addressed or talked about. Once you have explained one guy to your counselor, you have a new problem, and a new guy to explain in your next session.

"Now this is Joe, right? The CEO, correct?" asks Mr. Counselor.

"No, you're thinking of Josh. The really good guy I wish I could be into, but I'm just not," you tell him.

"Oh wait, who is Joe again? Who are Josh and Corey? You've also talked about an Alex and a Dillon. I'm so confused, here. I'm sorry sweetie. Blake and the boy next door are the only two I am able to keep straight. Please re-explain," he says.

Then by session three, you only talk about the new guy, who is of course gone by session four. You don't "pursue" this craziness, so why does this keep happening? Should you just stay locked up in your apartment without a phone or social media? Never mind…they always find a way to get to you. Pretty soon you realize your unpredictable life changes so quickly that just keeping the details straight, and trying to remember what components your counselor does and doesn't know, is causing you anxiety in itself. Do they prescribe Zoloft for anxiety that is caused in a counseling session where there is TOO much to talk about that cannot be addressed within the one hour? Probably not. The problem you are facing is that to have effective counseling, you would need your counselor to be with you 24/7, which he cannot do. You are already quite aware of the train wreck you are and the options available to you. You told Mama before you began that your biggest fear was that even a counselor couldn't help you? You were right, sista! Carry on!

As soon as you leave the office and tell your counselor that you are going to try to do things on your own for a while, lo and behold: You have a missed call from Corey! Say what? This guy won't be re-entering your life ever again…he's had one chance too many and, "Ohhhh, what's this?"

A text from…*drum roll*…Blake!! What's he asking this time? Oh, it's just another proposal to go elope in Vegas, and have kids with him immediately. That's all…no big deal. You get this text on a weekly basis. As usual, he will take it all back in the morning when he sobers up again.

Apparently their radar chips now even go off as you're leaving counseling:

"Houston, she has quit counseling! Confuse the heck out of her ALLLLLL over again. She is no longer paying to talk to anyone, so your chances of successfully making her pull out all of her hair have become increasingly higher!"

You turn around and say, "Counselor do you have five minutes?"

He points to the clock and says, "Sorry time is up."

Located next to the office, is the best bakery in town, and they have colossal triple death by chocolate cakes for only $10 today. They're so appealing, so uncomplicated, and so rich…unlike the guys you keep falling for. You're pretty sure you can pull off eating this heavenly baked good in the next few days. Perhaps you could have a friend over to share some with you? Okay no, who are you kidding? This is the kind of night where it will be devoured in one sitting. Oh well, your good intentions of doing otherwise count just a little. Okay, no, good intentions don't count at all. You are a sad mess, but at least you have chocolate cake to ease the pain….for tonight.

Harsh Leah Reality #13: New Year…Old Problems

Here it is another year. Remember last New Year's Eve how your man of the hour was in the bathroom during the ball drop? There you were, just sitting there all alone and all awkward. Everyone around you was sucking faces, while you felt the imaginary flashing neon arrows pointing straight at you. You knew from the beginning that having someone to spend that "magic moment" with was probably too good to be true…and you were right!

Well, this year, you don't even have a man anywhere near your presence to worry about. That's right…you're instead home alone lounging in your recliner chair, eating leftover Christmas chocolates, sipping on Welch's sparkling grape juice, and working on your expanding tush. Oh, and you're drinking your juice from a wine glass, of course…because that's your idea of living on the edge. Rather than thinking about your future husband or wondering if "Mr. Man of the Hour" is the one as you were last year, you're instead carefully planning your future as an old "cat lady." The good news? You even phoned a friend today that wants to join you on your early quest of "single old ladyism." Who says the Golden Girls can't start young? There isn't any kind of an age limit on this sort of thing now, is there? At least you have something to look forward to. Heck, they even have the seasons of your beloved favorite show on DVD now, and you all can watch it together, while you each cuddle with your furry friends.

In regards to the big New Year's Eve extravaganza though: You really did have intentions of going out with the "cool crowd," and wearing that too young for your late 20's, hip-hugging, off the shoulder sequin dress, and looking like you just stepped off the runway…or off the counter at a bar. You really planned on making a big hoopla out of everything and being a big city socialite in an attempt to completely rebel against last year, but you just don't have the energy. You have officially come to a point of acceptance. It's a new year, you're another year older, you don't have a new year's resolution, and you're not making one, because you know you won't keep it anyways. Same crap…different year, sister. You are no longer believing that you will have Mr. Right next year at this time. This upcoming year will probably just be a repeat of this year, but with a few minor changes, and a few temporary non-committing losers added to your dating roster. Other than that, things will pretty much be the same. No use in disappointing yourself with high hopes, right?

Besides, this is living. That $1.99 loaded with sodium canned beef stew from the discount store you just ate is probably better than the crockpot "champion chili" all your friends are eating at the parties you were invited to tonight…but didn't go to. Your meal of choice is especially probably better than the filet mignon and caviar that all the spoiled woman are picking at tonight in front of their dates at their downtown high dollar dinners. At least you can stuff your face, and do so in privacy.

Oh, and these sweatpants are amazing! Like seriously, who would want to wear a dress that is about to burst at the seams and make one struggle for air, when you can wear this loose, warm, and amazingly comfortable article of clothing? Oh, that's right…and it's SO cold out tonight. Who in the right mind would want to be walking the streets of downtown, shivering, and wearing next to nothing? Six inch stilettos didn't sound so fun tonight either. At least when you're kicked back in your recliner, you can't hurt yourself. Heck, even when you're walking around your massive 700 square foot apartment tonight, you are much less likely to fall in slippers. Well maybe not, since you are a bigger klutz than Anne Hathaway in "The Princess Diaries," but the point is: You are comfortable, you are warm, and you have no one to fight with tonight… because there is no one to ditch you at the bar to talk to the little slightly younger, slightly blonder thing, that has a dress slightly shorter, and slightly tighter than yours. You can go to bed drama-free without any arguments from anyone. Well except your parents of course, who will be phoning you later tonight, because of their concern that you might be on a path of life-long singleness. What do they mean "might?" You KNOW you are on that path.

So what if you don't have anyone to kiss at midnight? You'll be in bed by then anyways. That's another advantage to "singleism"…you go to bed whenever you want. If you had a boyfriend or husband, he would likely want to stay up for the ball drop, or even if he didn't, you would feel obligated to. No man = no obligations. Also, when you hit the hay for the night…you can sleep in the MIDDLE of the bed, and keep all of your covers on this cold, winter night. Granted your mattress is hard as a rock, and out of balance from the zero use that the right and left sides are receiving from the zero TLC you receive, but that is alright with you!

Also, that last glass of Welch's sparkling grape juice just before you drift off for the night at 9:30 p.m. sharp has such a nice refreshing zap to it, and you don't have to share it with anyone. Imagine if you had a man there with you…he may ask for a glass. Since you don't have to share, you can drink for two, sweetheart! Cheers to another year of no change and eternal singleness!

Harsh Leah Reality #14: Cougar Mama?

Months later, you entertain the idea of dating once again – but you're scared to think too long and hard about it. Rest assured someone else quickly comes your way. He definitely won't be your "usual" though…

When you were in high school, you had heard of the term "cougar," but at the time, all that term meant to you was the competing school's mascot. It also was the model of your cheerleading advisor's cool car.

"What exactly is a cougar?" you can remember innocently asking the girls in your friend circle one day.

"An older woman who dates younger men," they explained.

At the time, you said "ewww," and that you couldn't imagine dating a younger man. As a "stuck-on-yourself-senior," you couldn't possibly imagine so much as dating a junior. Well, that was then and this is now.

You are now in your later 20's, you're a bit jaded, and you're just not feeling as young as you once did. You can no longer eat "Cheez-Its" at 3 a.m. because of weight gain, and because you're simply now the type to hit the hay way before then. Also, attempting an old cheerleading stunt could now land you in the ER. You now use the facial moisturizer that your young looking mother has always sworn by, because your under-eyes are anxious to reveal some age lines. Your idea of a Friday night is watching Netflix in your pajamas and chowing down on your favorite pizza. "Surfing" now means flipping channels or playing on the web, rather than catching waves. Your metabolism is slightly different, you have mysterious aches and pains, you prefer flats over heels at times, and in terms of appeal, you're not entirely sure that "you still got it."

You're not currently succeeding at any relationships (which is breaking news to you and everyone else), but you are indeed crushing on someone. We're not just talking about a little crush here either. We're talking about full blown, hardcore massive crushing. You don't think you've felt this giddy about anyone since high school, and that's just the thing: He's only a couple years out of high school himself.

However, you get a massive ego boost about possibly snagging your latest crush, when you're informed by your little high school pal Stacy that you are the talk of her senior class.

"The boys in my class say *you've got it going on*," Stacy informs you.

No, you're not Stacy's mom like the "Fountains of Wayne" hit song…but you are nearing 30, and according to them, you've got it going on! That is enough for you.

It appears that you are more popular with Stacy's class than you were with your own back in the day, but that's okay. It's a much needed ego boost, even if it is ten years too late, and these guys are entirely too young for you.

As you're riding on the fact that high schoolers find you "hot," your Facebook message notification pops up. Hmmmm…Jacob, who just graduated from Stacy's school two years ago is raving about how beautiful you are, and how he wants to meet you in person. Aw, how sweet…when you were a senior, he was nine years old. When he was in Mommy's womb, you were learning multiplication facts, and when you were driving a car, HE was playing with action figures.

However, Jacob just happened to be the school's star quarterback two years ago. Now, he plays college football, and he's the "hot man" on campus, which is a bit intimidating in itself. However, from what you've heard from Stacy, he doesn't just randomly message girls.

"He's extremely picky, and he broke a lot of hearts in high school. He only dated the smartest and the prettiest," Stacy insists.

"Sweetie, he's eight years younger than me. He must not realize how old I am," you say.

"Actually he does know how old you are, because I told him, and he doesn't care. In fact, he finds it sexy that you're an older, stronger woman. He thinks you're one of the prettiest girls he's ever seen in his life. He's looking for maturity, stability, and a woman who knows what she wants," she continues.

"He may be of legal age for me…but that's about it. Heck, he's only 20…he can't even go into the bars with me for my songwriting events," you whine.

Nonetheless, Jacob's charm wins you over. Blame it on those blue eyes, his perfect physique, that southern drawl, and the fact that he looks JUST like your type. You accept his date offer. After all, nothing has worked out with any of the older guys – you've dated your own age all the way to ten years older, and everyone has proven to be the same. Your age is full of non-committers, and older guys are just plain set in their ways.

Maybe THIS guy is still trainable, and maybe you can mold him into the perfect guy? MAYBE younger is the new older. Maybe THIS guy will admire your independence because he's not really had to be independent all that long himself. Maybe this relationship could be less of a power struggle than your previous ones. Maybe.

You and Mr. Quarterback stay up talking all night, and you find out what it's like to kiss those perfect lips. He admits to you that he noticed you long before the Facebook message. He commented on Stacy's pictures with you previously, and confesses that he always had a massive crush on you. You admit that you once asked Stacy who that hottie was when you saw his picture. He says he's completely flattered that you would even consider him, and that he's even happier you agreed to a date. He asks you random facts about your life, and you ask him random facts about his. You feel like this date is going incredible, but in your cynical mind, you find yourself thinking: WOW...is something ACTUALLY going good for me? Surely SOMETHING is off? This guy is too hot and too young for his own good.

You were right, girl. So right. One month later, the sweet phone calls and texts come to an abrupt halt. You were special...you really were...along with his three other girls. Apparently he's also pursuing one of your so-called friends. You KNEW it was going to crash and burn. You're glad you were emotionally prepared, and that you had slapped yourself out of your "perfect positivity" early on. It has now been reaffirmed that positive pessimism is the way to go.

Stacy apologizes, and tells you that she NEVER saw this coming. Apparently Jacob is a multi-tasking player...and football isn't even his best game.

You tell yourself, you are definitely DONE with younger. Younger is trouble – they have no idea what they want, and they aren't mature enough to match up with you.

However, the 20-year-olds seem to be coming out of the woodwork these days…and it is still hard to resist. Maybe you just came across a bad apple? As the texts and Facebook messages continue, you wonder what is going on. Your little sister comments that young guys check you out as you walk through the grocery store, and your best friend calls you oblivious for "not noticing" the table of high schoolers that were eying you over lunch. You ensure her that you aren't oblivious…you are just trying to not draw attention to it. Lately, ZERO older guys seem to be interested in you, and it's maybe sort of bothering you. Maybe.

Are you getting a younger, high school-ish look suddenly?

Is there a new fad going on, in which younger guys want older women because they want a sugar mama to be the breadwinner while they sit at home and play video games all day?

Is this the best thing that has ever happened to you or the worst?

Do the older guys see you as competition for their own lives and careers?

What is going on?

You have no idea, but you aren't minding the ego boost…even if you know it's going nowhere fast. Hey, at least it is encouraging to know that the older you get, there is more of an age range gap that you apparently now have to choose from. Maybe you won't end up old and single. Maybe you will instead end up old and taken by a much younger man. Naw, probably not…being in *any* relationship just doesn't quite match your thinking these days.

Harsh Leah Reality #15: Showered with Showers & Unwanted Advice

Fast forward…your cougar stage is long over, but you are definitely getting older every day. You have begun to notice that every time you head to your mailbox, the only things waiting for you are bills, save the date magnets, and invites to showers, weddings, and parties. You find yourself wondering how many invites you can possibly receive from one person before they actually tie the knot or pop out a baby. From weddings, to showers, to bachelorette parties, to engagement gatherings, to baby gender reveals, to anniversaries, to parties that you didn't even know existed, your wallet is crying out for you to "STOP."

As you open your mailbox door, you think to yourself:

"Let's see, I've gotten ten announcements and or invites from this person...sooooo I guess that about covers it."

Of course your mailbox especially begins to overflow with these sorts of things right after a vicious, heart-wrenching breakup. The truth is, after your latest split, you'd rather hibernate at home than go out anywhere, much less to something like this. However, not only does your book of lame excuses for not attending only go so far, but you do want to be there for them, and you'd feel like a bad friend for not attending. Your heart just hurts right now, and this is all kind of adding insult to injury. Even though you're in the midst of a *very* late 20's crisis and you feel even more hopeless than you did at the last gathering full of pregnant and engaged women, you know you need to go.

On the very day that you find out your latest heartbreak has possibly found a new flavor of the week, you have to throw yourself together, and head to a friend's latest celebration. You've already been to her "I'm Pregnant" party, and now you're about to go to her "Gender Reveal" party. You're assuming that the next party is going to be her actual baby shower, but who knows at this point? Once you get through all the parties for this baby, baby #2 will likely be on the way, and then all the birthday parties will happen, and so on and so forth.

You awkwardly walk in alone to a room full of glowing faces, all of which you've never met before, except of course for the guest of honor. You take a seat on the sofa right by the food table. Mama Mia who is expecting her third baby plops down beside you, shakes your hand, and introduces herself. Although she is incredibly sweet, you lead completely different lives, and you're simply polar opposites. Beyond asking her about her children and the one on the way, you cannot for the life of you think of anything else to say to her. That's okay though, because once she found out you were single and kid-less, she decided to move on to baby-popping Brenda who she could better relate to. It all started with a diaper bag compliment, and then continued with breast-feeding talk.

You sit there thankful for your phone as it provides comfort in the constant socially anxious situations you find yourself in almost every weekend. As you sit there wondering when cake is going to be served, you get to hear a little bit of everything:

"Ohhh girl, I remember having those swollen ankles."

"When I had Aiden by c-section it was the way to go."

"I became a complete basket case during my third pregnancy, and my poor hubby stayed by my side every step of the way. I kicked him out of bed at night and sent him out on midnight grocery shopping trips to satisfy my cravings. I craved orange push-up pops and pork chops... all in one sitting!"

"That is so funny Shayla," exclaims Jenny. "I craved Reese's Pieces and butterscotch chips on my raspberry sherbet the entire pregnancy... and ohhhhh taco pizza with ketchup on it...I think that's how I put on all my weight."

In that very moment, you realize if pregnancy were contagious... you would be pregnant with at least triplets at this point.

Well, so you made an hour appearance, and now it is time for you to head to your other friend's wedding shower. (At least that's what you think this one is). Yep, that's right. Two back-to-back showers always happen during the time in which you feel like someone ripped your heart out of you and then ran over it, just to confirm that it was shattered and will never recover. When it comes to this friend, you've already attended her "I'm Engaged" party, and her "Wedding Detail Announcement" party, so you're admittedly kind of excited to be almost half way done. No offense to her, because you love her to death, but she's a bit of a Bridezilla. She seems like she could be the classic diva on TLC's "Say Yes to the Dress" with an unlimited budget, who turns down every single dress presented to her. You're pretty sure that you're going to be attending parties on a weekly basis for her marriage for at least a couple years. Then the countless baby parties will replace these bridal celebrations once the newness of their nuptials wears off.

This gathering is almost more problematic than your previous shower today, because THIS time, you are about to play the 20 questions game. You actually know most of the girls at this particular party. Also, you didn't tell these particular friends that Luke broke your heart last week and it looks as though he may already have a new flavor of the week. You're kind of tired of having to give constant updates to so many people that you can no longer keep track of who knows what and who doesn't. You have some friends who may even think you're still with that loser you were dating last year at this time, and by now, that was three guys ago. However, for those who knew about Luke, it is obvious that they STILL unfortunately think you are together. This ought to be real fun. You are likely to get as much attention as the bride-to-be. You do not consider this kind of attention to be a good thing at all.

Much to your surprise, you have made it through the first hour and a half without ANY questions. Your friends all seem to be so focused on Lily and Jason's engagement pictures that they barely notice that you're there, which you are perfectly okay with. You can handle all the chitter chatter about love and all the baby talk, so long as you aren't asked about your own personal life. Well, maybe you can't handle ALL the chitter chatter, because the next topic of discussion is about to rub you wrong.

You hold back the crocodile tears and bite your tongue as you hear Lily say that she and Jason's first dance will be to "When You Say Nothing At All." The Keith Whitley original version to be exact. Ummmm…you told her that it was going to be YOUR song someday, and it's all good and everything that she wants to use the same one, but it's just a bit of a dagger to your heart as just last week you were seriously imagining that being you and Luke's song. Yep, for a whole month, you had been thinking about the "what ifs" of you and him. However, now, your fantasies are about as realistic as the MASH game that you used to play in elementary school. No wait, the MASH result where you end up unmarried, with a beater car, poor, and living in the sewer, seems much more realistic to you right now actually.

You're still kind of stuck on the fact that you will soon be witnessing a first dance to the song that she hadn't even heard of until last week, when you hear…"We all know who is NEXT!"

"So when's your shower girly!? You've been seeing each other a few months. Isn't it time for him to propose?!"

"Oh, um, well, I don't think so," you nervously reply.

"Honey…," continues maid of honor Mindy. "I know that look on your face. Is there something you're not telling us?"

"Yeah, maybe there is," you answer. "Luke and I are history, but I'm okay. You know…I'm used to things not working out."

The room erupts with "what's," "when's," "where's, "why's," "how's," apologies, theories as to what went wrong, as well as predictions of your future, while you just shrug your shoulders, and assure the room that you're fine. You then wonder if you're trying to assure them you're fine or if you're trying to assure yourself. Okay, so maybe a little bit of both, but you don't want to talk about it anymore, and unfortunately the can of worms has been opened, and these girls know no limits. You know the blinding spotlight is on you, so you have to at least sort of explain what happened between the two of you. You give them the 30 second version. Apparently 30 seconds was all that everyone needed to make a diagnosis as to why your relationship failed.

"Sweetie," says bridesmaid Brittany…"I think you were too good for Luke. All I've gotta say is good riddance to him."

"I really think you would be soooo great with Brian that I want to introduce you to," contributes Mindy.

"I disagree," chimes in Candice. "I think her and Luke were perfect together. I believe he will be back."

"I believe he's going through a tough transition time with his new job and all. It's not hcr, it's him," adds Kristie.

"Have you considered online dating?" quizzes Anna. "A girl I work with just met her fiance' on E-Harmony, and they are perfect together!"

"You've always been too picky. I think it's time for you to be realistic and stop setting your standards so high," comments Cami.

"Your interests were just too different. I mean a country girl and a rap lover just don't work," insists Sarah.

"Girl, based on what you told me about his commitment phobia and his lack of affection towards you, I'm thinking Luke may not be attracted to women," adds Natalie.

"You don't know what you're talking about," Candice fires back. "You are definitely wrong about that. Their chemistry was undeniable. He just needs to mature a little," she continues.

Always Right Rhonda pops up with saying, "He's just not that into you. Sweetie, I know it hurts, but it's true. If he were, he would be with you right now."

"I think ALL of you are wrong," suggests Nikki. "I think there is another girl involved. Remember Luke did have trouble getting over Shelly."

You silently think about your suspicions of him and his new flavor of the week, realizing your guess is probably better than theirs, and that you could minimize their theories in 2.2 seconds, but you refuse to go there.

You find it amazing that they think ten different answers from ten different friends is something that you could actually find helpful. You know they mean well, but they have just worsened your already poor condition. You continue to listen, yet slightly drown it out as the conversation shifts back and forth from you, all the way back to their own lives.

"I think Deacon is going to propose super soon," says Natalie, the only other not engaged girl you knew of in the room. (Of course, most of them aren't just engaged…but married with a child or two…or three).

Always Right Rhonda says to you, "See darling. That is what you need - a guy who is truly into you. My husband Randy has always been into me. Deacon is clearly into Natalie, and that is why she is confident he will be proposing. Jason is into Lily, and that's why they are getting married super soon. Isaac is into Cami and that's why he just asked her to marry him. That is what you need. You need to be more open to meeting good guys. We watch you reject the good ones over and over again."

By the time you leave the shower, you feel like you want to go rob the nearest bar, and you don't even drink…at all.

Harsh Leah Reality #16: Going through the awkward wedding motions

Here it is all the way back to the month of "Jubilant June." Ah, it's the month of I Do's, cheesy speeches, saving the dates, awkwardly standing around for the bouquet toss, and being reminded of your singleness each and every weekend…sometimes at two different ceremonies a day. Maybe things will slow down in "Single September," and stay slow until "Fiancé February," when the Facebook newsfeed is flooded with all of the accepted proposals that will result in a future "Jubilant June" wedding. For now, all you're doing is going through the awkward motions. All you're trying to do is get through each and every weekend without someone trying to set you up with one of the "single for a reason," groomsmen.

How many times do you have to dance with someone you're just not digging?

How many times do you have to botch up the electric slide, and pray that they put on the 'Cha –Cha' or chicken dance instead?

Your uncoordinated and mediocre sheltered child dancing abilities just don't allow for much else detail.

Once again, you feel that those flashing neon arrows have *singled* you out. Sigh……

During yet another bouquet toss in which they call all the single ladies to the floor, you realize you are now the oldest. While your adult arms stand a better chance of catching the bouquet than the six to twelve year olds who you share the floor with, you let them fight it out and have their moment. After all, the person who catches it should be getting married next…and at this rate, you feel like the six year old missing her two front teeth has a better chance of beating you to the altar. You first try to avoid the toss, but of course everyone tells on you, and the DJ announces that you better get your butt up there. You really should have hidden in the bathroom…but then, everyone would probably know you were trying to bail, and the DJ would have announced that they were waiting on you to get your potty break done. When you just can't win…you give in.

After pretending that you actually put effort into the bouquet toss, you realize that if life were the freakin' movies, the man of your dreams would walk up to the bridal table you're sitting at once again and ask you to dance. Better yet, he would have swept you up off your feet from that "single ladies' floor," you were standing on. Can't this AT LEAST be "My Best Friends' Wedding," where even just a guy friend comes to rescue you? No it can't, sweetie. This is not the movies, so in reality, you will probably just have to suck it up, and make it through the night… alone. That's real life for ya!

Harsh Leah Reality #17: Your Ex = Dream Stealer

Ever since you can remember, you have ALWAYS wanted a Camaro. While other girls were begging Daddy for another Barbie, you were begging Daddy to take you to the Chevy lot so you could scope out the Camaros. Daddy always assured you that if he were a rich man, he would buy you that Camaro, but the fact is: He is not a rich man.

Fast forward to 20-something years later into your movie-like life which is much more like a horror film than a chick flick. You are working your unfulfilling, dead-end job in which you can barely pay the rent, and you are driving a four-door boring economy car and just feeling kind of "blah" in most areas of life. You've recently endured the Luke breakup, but at least you finally paid off your boring car. It only took you six years and cost you $2,500 in repairs this year. You are kind of feeling content with paying something off for the first time, because of all the hard work, blood, sweat and tears that it took to do so. However, your achievement celebration is incredibly short-lived as your ex-boyfriend soon bursts your bubble.

Throughout your time of dating Luke, you always revealed your biggest hopes and dreams to him. He was just easy to open up to like that. You told him about your dreams of broadcasting for a major news network, having the home with the porch that wraps all the way around, and last but certainly not least…owning a Camaro. While supportive of your dreams, Luke was always trying to assure you that Camaros were really not that great.

"Dodge Chargers are much cooler," he would always tell you.

"I just can't agree with you. I'd take a Charger, but for me, there is just something about a Camaro. I will own one someday…mark my words," you insisted.

Well, you really shouldn't have marked your words or even told him what you wanted to begin with, because six weeks after Luke admits he isn't ever going to marry you or anyone…HE goes and buys a brand spanking new, high speed, luxury everything…Camaro, with features that you didn't even know existed. He proudly posts pictures of it on his Twitter account and brags like it's his job.

"Say what," you ask yourself?

"Really…I mean REALLY…why did he feel the need to choose a CAMARO out of all the numerous choices he had!? Especially when a month ago…he didn't even like them! Was it just to spite me!? Did he do this just because he has more money than me!? This cannot be a coincidence when we had this talk all the time, and he acted like he didn't like them!!"

Not even an unrealistic chick flick and a tub of cookie dough will nurse this wound. No, it won't! Off to the car lot you go! You don't care if you can afford that CORVETTE! YOU WILL OWN IT BY THE END OF THE DAY! You pay no mind to the fact that if your current car broke down you couldn't even afford to repair it, let alone buy an expensive new car. Yep, that's right…you've switched from a Camaro to a Corvette, and nothing is going to stop you from driving it off the lot. You wanted a Camaro, but now you've got to outdo Luke no matter what the cost is. Camaros are still so beautiful, but you have to go a step above him now. Sure he makes a six figure sum yearly, and you barely make above the poverty line, but you have GOT to HAVE IT.

After sitting down with the salesman, he assures you he could give you $2,000 for your trade-in. You then try to inform him that Kelley Bluebook value says $5,900. He tells you that your asking price is simply not realistic, nor is you affording a Corvette to begin with. He recommends that if you want a different kind of car, you may consider the used minivan in their lot instead – because it's in your price range. You ask him if he is insulting your intelligence, your credit score, and your bank account. You then tell him you only want a Corvette. For one of the first times in car sales' history, the dealer turns the customer away. It was worth a try...You officially feel like Annie in "Bridesmaids"... because of your embarrassing beater car AND your relationship status.

Harsh Leah Reality #18: Another One Bites the Dust

So now, you're on the way to the hair salon. You're a dark blonde and you can't wait to get a trim and a new sun-kissed blonde style for the summer. You don't desire anything too drastic. You just want to feel more like a Baywatch babe, but you're a traditionalist. Granted Luke likes dark-haired exotic girls, but you're no longer living to please him. You just like to look crisp, clean, tanned and refreshed. You can't wait to just get there, catch up with your stylist, kick back, and relax. You're stuck in traffic for well over an hour, and you're a bit tired, and a bit out of it when all of the sudden...your little sister Lauryn, who is riding shotgun, shrieks that classic freak out sound which almost sends you wrecking your car into the naked statue in the busiest part of downtown.

"WHAT!?" you ask her scared out of your mind.

"I think Luke got married...this is insane," she yells.

"Shut up!" you say in complete and utter disbelief.

"No really," she insists…"Look at the Facebook photo and the caption!"

You're trying to convince yourself it's a joke, especially since you only ended things with him two months ago, with him claiming he never wants to get married. Also, this chick looks opposite of his type, but if it's a joke, they're playing it off WAY too well. This is the ultimate shocker, and has cruelly blindsided you even worse than your last pathetic relationship coming to an end. They both look drunk out of their minds, and he's been known to make crazy, unexpected impulsive decisions while under the influence. You look closer, and see that they even got hideous matching wrist tattoos, saying "Kassie and Luke forever."

As you enter the salon, your mind is in a chaotic blunder as you explain to your stylist Shannon what you think just happened. "Whoa, wait, WHAT!?," she asks. "Luke, as in the Luke I met a couple months ago?"

"Yes, him," you manage to say as if you're about to hyperventilate.

"Shut up!…That is insane! I think you need a whole new look today if this Facebook crap is true," she adds.

"I want jet black hair…the blackest you have," you say without hesitation. Then I want you to add a pink streak, and I want you to chop six inches off, and turn this into a chin cut!! Then after I leave the salon, I'm thinking about getting my first tattoo, and my first piercing besides my ears."

"Whoa, hold on a second," Shannon replies. "Does this jet black hair in the middle of the summer have ANYTHING to do with Luke?"

You give her that guilty smile, knowing that she is most definitely not going to let you do something so ridiculous just to impress your sorry ex. She then proceeds to mix up the blondest concoction you've ever seen, and assures you that it would feel best to go completely opposite of the color that your ex likes.

"Don't make a long term decision on a temporary feeling," she says.

You agree, and as you're sitting under the dryer letting your color sink in, your friend John calls you. This is a call you must take, whether under the noisy hair dryer or not. You take the call, pull your head out from under the dryer, throw down that Cosmo magazine that is giving you false hope in men, as your sister insists that you must put your head back under. As John confirms that what you are seeing on Facebook is indeed true, you find yourself yelling loud enough for the whole salon to hear.

Apparently her wedding attire consisted of yoga pants and a tube top, while he sported plaid pajama pants and the shirtless look. His drunken friend Lenny, who has no business being an ordained minister officiated the ceremony on the bar patio. You bet they didn't make the best dressed section of that Cosmo magazine you were just reading. Now that reality has set in, and they've somewhat sobered up, they're discussing whether or not they should annul their marriage.

You realize that alongside a bar, tattoo parlor, car dealership, and mall, a salon is probably the worst place you could be at a time like this, because it has to do with your image, which he for some reason didn't appreciate. While you didn't get your jet black hair, you chop your long locks up to your chin. You then decide to then treat yourself to EVERYTHING that the salon offers – including a facial, an eyebrow waxing, and every upscale hair product known to man. You then proceed to buy a new flat iron, makeup, accessories, and pretty much any and every product the salon carries.

As your bill rings up to $500, even your stylist says "Wow this is the most you've EVER spent in here."

You say, "Yeah, you're right…but I've got another $1,500 which can go towards the Corvette and house I'm heading to check out next! The dealer said "no" on that Corvette I wanted last time, but he won't say "no" this time! Just wait and see!"

Your little sister shakes her head and says, "Maybe I should stay in town with you another week sis…"

Harsh Leah Reality #19: Online Dating & Tortuous Waiting

Okay, so it looks like it's time to scratch Luke off the list for good. You still talk to the boy next door and Blake still feels the need to call you just to confuse you on a weekly basis. Nonetheless, you have got to move on with life, and you want to do so with a guy who wants what you want. Your friends keep insisting you are popular among the male world and that your pickiness is ruining everything. What to do…what to do?

Well, remember how you swore off online dating? Yes, yes you do…and you especially can't deny that you wound up giving in. After counting that you have nine ex-boyfriends, you realize that if #10 doesn't work out, you will have run out of fingers, and let's face it: If you run out of fingers…you're definitely doomed, never getting married and dying alone. None of your past approaches have worked. Perhaps this one will…or perhaps it won't…like usual. What do you have to lose at this point? Well, nothing except the fact that it may cause you to run out of fingers and be forever doomed…absolutely nothing.

Despite your skepticism, you figure that you might as well give it a whirl. You're still mildly scarred from your friend Lindsay's nightmare experience. For two weeks, she thought she was talking with the CEO of a big company who also was supposedly the owner of a BMW. Turns out, her prospect was the CEO of his parent's basement, and the passenger in a wood-paneled station wagon, in which his mother chauffeured him to the date in. Lindsay knew she had spotted "Waldo" stepping out of Clark Griswold's old car the second she laid eyes on him. She was also shocked that he chose to mark the 6' 4" "athletic build" description on his profile, when he was really more like 5' 5" and "more to love." Just tell the truth, dude! After all the deceit, she couldn't even give your personality a try!

Surprisingly, as you're browsing the site for "free" with no intention of joining, you see a photo of someone who actually sparks your interest. Say it isn't so - your typical out of your reach type actually exists on online dating sites? You thought dating sites were only for expedited, under the gun dating, but it looks as though you just may have been wrong to assume. Something about this guy screams "slightly hard to get," whereas so many of the other profiles scream "desperation." That vibe alone makes you want this guy...badly.

It isn't long before your inbox is filling up with desperate men who seemingly would marry anything on two legs. You are still waiting on a message from "that one" who caught your attention, but not surprisingly, he has said nothing...though everyone else and their brother has contacted you. In the meantime, the ONLY other user besides him that you had interest in contacts you, and he puts the name of your HOME STATE of Kentucky as his subject, but you can't actually read anything else or respond to him unless you pay to join. Of course...it's a money trap. Ahhh...and now, he is sending you "chat requests." You can't respond to those either.

Sigh...okay, okay. No one has to know that you've caved and given in. Once you find out this guy is a loser who only contacts you sporadically, you'll go back to your original skepticism. Once you learn that he has been lying about everything under the sun, including his wife and three kids located in another country that need their green cards, you'll simply deactivate your account, right? Right.

So many of the other profiles sending you messages make you want to place up your defenses and delete your account that you've been on a for a whole two seconds. Starting out a profile with, "Near or far...I'll go wherever you are," is just kind of a deal breaker for you. You aren't supposed to feel smothered before you even meet a person. You haven't even spoken to this guy, and you can tell he's worse than the static cling on that dress you keep swearing you're going to give to the Goodwill. He puts in the headline of the e-mail that he is willing to move the 2,000 miles to get to you, and says in the first line of his e-mail that you'd made a great wife and mother. Dude has never met you...how does he know if you have good domestication skills or that you know the first thing about parenting? Furthermore, why does he think you're so automatically ready to pick out curtains and car seats with him? You're just not feeling it...and you never will.

Nothing can beat the 66-year-old who messaged you and said "You're cuter than a ham sandwich…and a ham sandwich looks pretty good to me!" You're not sure what's worse: The fact that he's twelve years older than your daddy or his pitiful pickup line?

Nonetheless, you are now able to reply to Mr. College Athlete from your home state. He is seemingly super into you, and you're starting to think that just maybe this online dating stuff actually works… sometimes. After all, you just need to find ONE man on there. You don't have to want EVERYONE on the site, right? You did your research on him, and his photos match up with the ones he texts you. He doesn't strike you as an ax murderer, nor does he seem annoyingly desperate. The guy wants to meet you, and though you feel that he is trying to meet you a little sooner than you are ready for, he has definitely captivated you.

For days, he continues to initiate conversation and to woo you via text message. He wants to make sure that he's the only man you're talking to, and can't wait for that first date with you. Suddenly, in the midst of a completely normal conversation that seems to be running smoothly as usual, he goes completely "cold turkey" and stops texting. It's just "crickets" from then on. You show the conversation to a guy friend, and ask him if you said anything wrong. He insists you didn't say anything wrong, and Mr. College Athlete is probably just yet another one of those flakes that you're so good at finding. Two weeks go by, and you find yourself still wondering what caused this guy to run. If this demise is your fault, you at least want to know your errors for future reference. You know it's against your usual rules to text any guy not treating you with the utmost respect, but you have GOT to know what this dude's problem is, or what YOUR problem is. You text him, and ask him why he randomly stopped texting you and why he has never contacted you again.

Much to your surprise, he quickly texts back, tells you how beautiful you are, how busy he's been, and that he most certainly hasn't forgotten about you. You are completely confused by his response as any guy who has true interest in a girl should never just stop texting for weeks.

You are especially confused since he was initially so insecure about the possibility of so many other guys seeing your profile and contacting you. Doesn't he know that online dating can get competitive if you don't stay on your toes?

"Well, I've just been so confused honestly. You suddenly stopped talking to me, and I haven't heard from you in weeks," you reply.

"Yes, you have, girl! I texted you on New Year's remember?"

Knowing that New Years was four days before and knowing that he didn't contact you that day or any day recently, you realize that you may in fact have run across yet another "female juggler." However, you set your suspicions aside for just a second. Obviously online daters may talk to a few people at once, but could this guy actually forget you? Is there another explanation? Did his text not come though? Still, what would his excuse be for ignoring you days prior to that? You talked in depth for a good while. Wouldn't that remain in his memory at least?

"I didn't get a text from you on New Year's," you reply.

"Oh man! I totally texted you! It must not have gone through," he insists. "Besides I didn't want to bother you too much. I knew you were on your way back from Dallas."

Ah-ha! You had your answer right then and there. You did not receive a text on New Year's, and you have never ever been to Dallas. The dots had all connected. He totally mixed you up with someone else. You had managed to find yet another jerk…one you had never even met in person! He couldn't even keep his online prospects straight.

Your response: "Dear Player, If you're gonna play the game, at least remember all the names." Signed, I don't travel to Dallas…EVER.

The craziest part? He acted like it was all a mistake and that he KNEW who you were. He tried to smooth things over, and started bringing up facts about you…things that you had told him. You let him know that he was only digging himself into a deeper hole, and he should probably move along with his new girl (who he had apparently ignored for the last four days as well).

Yeah, this star basketball player definitely missed the slam dunk, dropped the ball, and fell right on his butt.

Remember that guy before "Mr. College Athlete" that had sparked your curiosity? He has FINALLY messaged you. You seem to immediately hit it off, and before you know it, you're talking on the phone. You meet, you hang out, and you get to know one another a bit. He's cute, he's smart, he's driven, but you don't feel any emotional connectivity to him. What's new, right? You only feel the magic connectivity with inaccessible jerks. Not to worry, it completely dies out somewhere shortly after date two. You feel apathetic about it all. Oh well, back to the drawing board. You were never really all that invested to begin with. As much as you wanted a "You've Got Mail" kind of story, it doesn't appear to be in the cards for you. Then again…you just never know.

Harsh Leah Reality #20: Facebook: The Accidental Friend Request

As many of us know, "Facebook" can unintentionally be a toxin for friendships and relationships nowadays, but unless you either:

A. Have the ability to resist the peer pressure of updating everyone on what you're eating for dinner, or when you're bored out of your mind, you're likely on there.
B. Unless you simply actually have a life unlike 99% of us that spend too much time on there, you are most likely partly on there because you cannot resist the nagging temptation of being a face-stalker from time to time.

Yes, none of us want to admit it. The fact that your ex-boyfriend's new girlfriend cannot tell you are face-stalking her public page thrills you. The fact that you can look up her every move without her realizing how very updated she keeps you, makes you feel slightly rebellious, and edgy…in a shamelessly geeky and perhaps creepy way. Not to mention, it reminds you of why you keep yours private.

You feel twice as rebellious that your ex himself has left his page public, even though you deleted him as a friend with no intention of re-adding him a long time ago. The feel-good deletion took place right after the breakup, of course! This wasn't just any short-term kind of anger delete either; this was a permanent, set in stone, "I'm done with you for good" removal. You were so pleased with yourself the day you deleted him that you even took a picture of the deleting moment, and sent it to your best friend Cara, who said she was so proud of you for doing so.

However, since he has kept his page public, this gives you twice the possibility of finding out their daily nonsense. You're still going to look at his stuff, but you don't want to give him the satisfaction of knowing you actually still look at his stuff. The deletion was supposed to imply that you no longer need to read any of his crap, and that you no longer have any use for him on your friend's list or in your life. True, you don't actually miss him. In fact, you think he's a loser at life. Maybe that's why you have FINALLY taken a whole week off from face-stalking him, though you're sure your curiosity will cause you to resume soon. It's just not worth your time this week.

Sadly for you, Cara gets just as much of a kick out face-stalking them as you do. The difference? She isn't taking the week off, and you actually WATCH what you're doing when you're investigating. You are a careful, cautious, face-stalker making sure to not "click" on anything that will blow your cover. She is not. Her fingers are recklessly clumsy, and she has been known to accidently "like" dark and gloomy, "I hate my life" kind of statuses. She just plain makes embarrassing mistakes as she is so quickly scrolling through the newsfeed starving for useless information. Sadder for you? She doesn't have an iPhone, so she is therefore, beyond obsessed with yours. Way, way sadder for you? You stayed logged in on your Facebook, and as usual, she's playing with it. You're kind of used to her being fascinated with your usually uneventful newsfeed activity, but you're not thinking of how potentially dangerous your sweet, sharing, and taking your turn nature is.

Fast forward to the next morning…you are thoroughly enjoying one of those exceptionally rare, beautiful princess sleeps, when you are awaken by a "ding." Hmmm…you have a Facebook notification.

That's nothing too unusual as you're so much "cooler online." Someone probably just likes the picture you posted of the calorie-istic cookies you baked last night. Perhaps someone wrote on your wall? Maybe the guy you're not interested in sent you a fifth private message this week? Another likely possibility? You got an annoying game request to go fight a fictional battle or something. Barely awake, you hit that beautiful blue "F" icon that you love so much…expecting for something totally non-life changing to appear, so that you can just roll over and go back to sleep. Your eyes go from Droopy the dog to Tweety Bird spotting a puddy tat within 0.5 seconds.

"Joe Limburtony" has now accepted your friend request!? Say what!?!?!?! You would NEVER EVER request him again. Someone couldn't pay you to do so, yet he evidently got a request from you! You are shaking and you are upset, wondering what in the world has happened. You begin assuming that a hater has hacked your account, or that you did something when you were practically dead for the night. Two seconds later, you realize you have your culprit! You realize Cara did this, and she better have a death wish, because you're fixing to show her your crazy side!

Cara, who slept in your guest room for the night, looks like she's having a princess sleep of her own, one that she most definitely no longer deserves. You storm and stomp as loudly as you can into that bedroom disturbed beyond belief, and upon grabbing the closest pillow, you knock her upside the head. You call her an "idiot," and tell her she isn't allowed to touch your iPhone ever again. She slowly opens her eyes, clearly not in tune with what is going on at all!

"You re-requested Joe on Facebook, you crazy, reckless moron! And he was dumb enough to actually accept!"

"Do you know what this DOES to me?" you continue. It makes Joe think I'm still stuck on him when I wouldn't date him ever again… even if he were the last man on the earth."

"I didn't do it!" Cara snaps back.

"Yes! You had to have done it! I've taken a week off from my stalking, remember?" you defend. "You were on my account last night, and we both know you have zero control over your fingers. Your auto corrects are the worst, you make people cry by liking statuses about having the worst days of their lives, you've lost friends by typing and entering a super rude status comment that you didn't intend to actually post, and you have written on the wrong walls before! Let's face it...it's YOU!!"

"We don't even know if it's me. I might be getting blamed for something I didn't even do," Cara whines.

"Were you on Joe's page last night?" you ask.

"Yea, I was…but I didn't request him," she insists.

"Oh okay…it just magically happened then," you sarcastically assure her.

"What am I gonna do!? It's gonna look stupid if I delete, re-add, and then delete again," you complain.

"I'm even already seeing pictures pop up in my newsfeed of half-dressed girl's photos that he's clicking "like" on again. I do NOT want to see this again. He annoys me, and I'm likely to make a hateful comment that'll make him cry like a little boy," you emphasize.

"Delete him off your newsfeed," Cara suggests.

You call her an idiot one more time, and realize that if you delete him again, she will just accidently re-add him from your page yet again, which will make a bad situation even worse. Then, you both burst out laughing, as laughing is all you can do at this point. You can feel your "crazy person laugh" unleash…the one you've had the past few years since your reality TV show drama began. You then proceed to laugh even harder imagining what his face must have looked like upon receiving your request. You reach the peak of your "crazy person laughter" as you are picturing him reluctantly accepting. It is during embarrassing moments like these when you realize that you're still alive, kicking…and miserably failing at keeping your dignity with your exes. The worst part is that it's your friend's fault, and there is nothing you can do to correct it. It wasn't even a choice you made, though that is what Joe obviously thinks. There is nothing you can do, nor explain. It would be worse explaining it was a "mistake request" which your friend did from stalking his page. There is nothing you can do except laugh, laugh, laugh until your sides are killing you…

You guess since he is now your friend again, now is the time to post pictures of you in that hip hugging mini skirt that he loved, or perhaps an album full of hot guys you met the other night, but don't actually know. The possibilities are endless and priceless. Thanks to Cara for breaking your four months of not associating with him record! Thanks a lot, pal!

Harsh Leah Reality #21: The Left Hand Ring Trend

Remember your high school prom? Of course you do…you talked about it earlier in the book, Miss Forgetful. Remember the "Dance the Night Away" story? Then again, your memory just isn't what it used to be. Okay, so you do recall it faintly. You even remember the "back-in-the-day happy couples" who shared a table with you that night. The night was young and so were you. You thought it was going to last forever, and you also thought those couples would last forever too, right?

Well, very few of them made it to the altar together. However, give or take a few failed relationships here and there, those same people for the most part ended up married, though it was to different people than you may have originally expected. Not only are they married, but they're popping out babies left and right everywhere you turn. So many of them are on kid three or kid four and you're not even in a relationship. Every other Facebook status and update is either about a wedding, a sweet hubby or kids, or of course a new baby on the way.

You have officially gotten to the point where you can barely have a conversation with any of your peers without hearing the dreaded "M" or "W" words. Now just to clear any possible confusion on the matter up: M and W does not stand for Monday and Wednesday in this case. In this lovely book, "M" & "W" of course stands for none other than "marriage" and "wedding." Ah, yes. You want to be so happy for them: All 900 of them. You really do! But, are you? Yes, of course you are!

Or…well, you're happy for them, but perhaps a little "indifferent" or "numb" could be a better word for it. They deserve happiness, as do you, but why are you the one having the bad luck?

Even the most unpopular people from your younger days have seemingly found their soul mates. You get their picture perfect family Christmas cards with a new baby picture each year, and of course, they're all in matching sweaters. You read their yearly recap letter which talks about their annual summer trip to the beach, in which this time they're all wearing white shirts and khakis, and they go on and on about coaching, PTA, gymnastics and piano lessons. As you read their letter, you're wondering…where is time going?

"Should I be learning how to make pretty cards, going to recipe exchanges, knitting scarves and above all, should I be learning what it means to be a domesticated woman?"

"Should I start thinking about being a wife and a mother?"

"If I poke around much longer are these people going to be grandparents before I'm a parent?"

You assure yourself single is good at this point…single is right for YOU. Maybe single is not right for them…but it is for YOU. But then at the most opportune time, "Enthusiastically Engaged Emily" and "Glowing Gloria" have to plop that Bridal magazine down on the table where you're sitting during lunch break. Your entire hour lunch break covers everything from the style of all the wedding parties' wardrobe to the centerpieces at the reception.

"I thought I wanted a mermaid dress but then I tried on a ball room gown, and my mom started crying and said, Oh Emily…you look like a princess. The most beautiful princess I've ever seen!"

"Oh Emily!..How Sweet!," comments Gloria…and then she continues, "When Jeff proposed to me, he said nearly the same thing, and I cried so hard. It was such a beautiful moment!!"

And there you are, taking it all in, trying to be supportive, truly being happy for them, but wondering where the heck do you fit in at this awkward time in life? You can't really contribute to the conversation when you're not married, engaged or even dating at this point. In fact, your current closest scenario to having a man is your nightly daily calls from the telemarketer that bears the name of Antoine. Antoine talking to you about free home estimates and lower interest rates unfortunately just isn't cutting it for you. His offers bore you, his voice isn't that sexy, and you hang up on him every night. Not a love story…a good one anyways. Despite your cynicism you're looking for something real like Gloria and Emily have found, but why aren't you finding it?

Quite honestly, you're officially getting kind of tired of hearing:

"When you know…you know!"

"I knew my hubby was the one from the first date and he felt the same about me.."

"It comes along when you're least expecting it!"

"Everything happens for a reason!"

Harsh Leah Reality #22: Flying Solo

So yeah…you've been feeling extra awkward about your singleness lately. You've made a deal with yourself that you're going to spend a little less time on the Facebook newsfeed…again. Anyways, it's time to fly home to see your family for the holidays. Of course you're flying solo, both literally and metaphorically. Therefore, you awkwardly stumble through the airport and onto the plane doing the penguin walk as you handle way too much luggage. You prefer the window seat, but this time you are stuck sitting in the middle seat, between two girls. After realizing you're too tired to read that book you have brought along about "growing old alone," you begin having light convo with the girl to your right. She says you look familiar, but when you say your name is Leah Gardowski, it is obvious that her mind goes blank. Still though, she is as sweet as can be, and you begin talking about your jobs and basic everyday stuff. You're from the same area! How cool.

Then comes the, "So do you have a boyfriend or husband?" question.

"Uh, nope. Completely single. Do you?" you ask.

"Yes, actually I'm engaged."

You smile and manage to offer her a true "congratulations," but within you, you're thinking…"Wow I really am the odd girl out. Maybe I should have opened that book after all, since apparently I'm the only single person still out there."

She continues by saying that she and her honey will be getting married in six months, and that most of the wedding planning has been done. Sincerely wanting to be supportive, you even ask her how she met her fiancé. For a second though, the conversation first shifts to your dreaded age.

"How old are you?" she asks.

"31," you say somewhat embarrassed by your single-as-you-can-get status.

"How old are you?" you ask.

"22," she says with a gigantic smile.

Ouch, just another reminder that you're way behind your peers.

Pretty soon the girl to your left pipes up for the first time on the plane ride, and excitedly asks your new flyer buddy:

"Did you say you're getting married!? I just got married two months ago! Oh my gosh! I'm loving married life. You're gonna love it! I'm so happy for you!"

Before you know it, you're managing your painfully fake smile, sipping your coffee, awkwardly lodged in between two sweet glowing girls and aspiring housewives. Meanwhile all you do is stare at your chipped fingernail polish and callused hands, realizing you've been anything but "taken care" of in life. Those flashing neon arrows from New Year's Eve and the single ladies' dance floor are back again. They're pointing straight at you, and they're declaring that you are "awkward and eternally single…" Where's "The Wedding Singer" when you need him? Never mind sweetie, you're not Drew Barrymore.

Harsh Leah Reality #23: The Old Maid of Honor

Remember how you were worried about being the MAID of Honor (not Matron) in your baby sister's wedding. Well, that fear is becoming a reality...at least it's leading to becoming a reality. Lauryn is doing better at 21 than you are at 31...but it is okay, really...you're just a late bloomer. Nick, the latest guy in her life has been saying things to her at 21 that no one has ever said to you. You may have changed this little girl's diapers, and she may have been just three feet tall when you brought home your first boyfriend that didn't work out over a decade ago...but you'll be okay. She could've been the flower girl at YOUR wedding...then she could've been your junior Maid of Honor...then she could have been your Maid of Honor...However though, it is looking like YOU will be the MAID of honor in HER wedding...which has become so much more than just a bridal title. You are turning into an old maid...quite literally.

Despite your slight insecurities which have now escalated into major insecurities, you begin planning her big day with her. Yes, that's right... he proposed to her while you were home in Kentucky on break. You are now the only single Gardowski out of seven children. You are awkwardly lodged in the middle...like usual. Yes, you have already been through five sibling weddings, and this one will make your sixth and final.

Anyways, Nick is a few years older than Lauryn, already owns a house, and is insisting that she follow whatever dreams she may have while he works hard to provide for her. After she gave him a resounding "yes," he gave her an authentic Coach purse, gift cards to the spa, and the keys to a brand new Mustang. What did you get out of the deal? You earned the "title" you were planning on earning of course.

As you begin flipping through the dreaded bridal catalogs, Lauryn says, "I'm so glad you're my Maid of Honor."

"Me too, sweetie," you reply.

"Yeah, I mean…with you being Maid of Honor, it won't be a big deal if your dress is different than the other bridesmaids. You looking different than everyone else will be perfectly acceptable," she says.

"What do you mean," you ask.

"Oh…you know. You're 31. I get it, Leah. You're not 20 anymore. Sleeves and a high neckline for you are totally okay with me…seriously. In fact, I'd feel most comfortable with you being the extra conservatively dressed one up there. I don't want you to feel the pressure of keeping up with my college-aged bridesmaids, and frankly, it'd be a little embarrassing if my older sister tried to dress "too young" up there. So go ahead and pick out some cute but comfy flat shoes, and you don't have to wear that flower in your hair like the other girls," she insisted.

"Gee, thanks sis," you respond.

"You're very welcome. Love you bunches and bunches," she replies without any idea she just shrunk your self-esteem by three sizes.

Oh well, at least she still loves you bunches and bunches, which is what you used to tell her as you tucked her into her little bed each night after reading her favorite bedtime story…Clearly, she took those fairy tales to heart. Sigh…you feel like Jane in "27 Dresses" yet again, except you don't actually want Nick. You're done being a cougar, and you're way above stealing your little sister's boyfriends. You do kind of wish Nick had a single brother though..

Harsh Leah Reality #24: Home videos = the new depressant

Speaking of your sister Lauryn, how about those times when you go home for a visit and she just HAS to pop in those old home videos? It's especially awesome when she chooses your brother Eric's wedding that happened a good twelve years ago, prior to he and your sister-in-law Ally's four children, and everyone growing up and changing way too fast. You were a bridesmaid with frizzy hair back then. Typical of your usual madness, you had your boyfriend at the time there, along with your ex-boyfriend who just happened to be sitting three rows behind.

So here we are all these years later, and pretty much everything and everyone has changed, except the fact that you are still unmarried and kid-less. Well not just unmarried but single…so yeah, something did sort of change actually. At least in the video you had a boyfriend, which is a whole heck of a lot more than you can say for yourself now.

After reminiscing over a long gone past, Lauryn turns back the clock even more. She begins playing the videos from your childhood. You know the ones where you had braided pigtails and you were missing your two front teeth? You were chasing around kitty cats that have been dead for a good two decades, and you were walking your beloved family dog that left your young life way too soon.

Styles have changed dramatically, but you kind of envy the old you: The girl who had the porcelain dolls in her room, the posters of Jonathan Taylor Thomas on her walls, and the albums of TOP baseball cards. You also couldn't help but miss the girl who showed off her Fisher Price kitchen and play food to the camera. You can't believe you actually enjoyed cooking at one time. Now you've grown into a woman that doesn't even want to cook real food. You especially envy the fact that you used to wear those pink jogging suits, those candy bar logo t-shirts and high top Reebok Velcro shoes. There is a clip of you making Barbie and Ken kiss on their wedding day and then driving them away in their Ferrari. You had decided they would spend their honeymoon in Malibu. It was when you believed that you were a Barbie and Ken story waiting to happen. It was the simple days. It was long before the heartbreaks, long before the drama and long before you realized that the relationship world isn't necessarily kind.

After a day of watching these videos, partly because you were too lazy to get up, and partly because you thought a look back might help your current condition for some reason, an almost dark cloud invades you. If one were to play your whole life by video now, they could now fast forward it to the part where you're officially looking into getting a Zoloft prescription to deal with the depression that the flashbacks have caused. Sigh…sometimes you just can't go home again.

Harsh Leah Reality #25: When Anesthesia Starts Talking

Fast forward.. Remember that time you had rhinoplasty surgery following your broken nose, and they put you under anesthesia? Well, you remember hearing about it afterwards, but you don't remember the crazy things that you apparently did while under the delusional outing. Prior to the surgery, you were warned you might wake up loopy. Being the tough kind of person who usually defies the normalcy of the recovery process, you weren't too worried about going under. Painkillers? You're not a wimp. Anesthesia? You've been under it before, and you woke up like a boss. For someone like you, this whole process is going to be a piece of cake, right?

After a detailed two hour surgery, you wake up and sit right up.

"Oh my goodness," shrieked your nurse. "Honey, we need you to lie back down. You've just been through a very major surgery, and you're going to have to be extra careful with your head for at least six weeks."

The first thing you think of?

"I wonder if my fiancé got me flowers?" (Of course he didn't, because once again…this isn't the movies. This is real life, and together you two take the term "dysfunctional" to a whole new level. Not only that, but you and Blake broke up a month ago. Yes – THAT Blake. After years of utter chaos, he proposed to you for real, and you said yes for real. Too bad, the engagement was broken off within a month. You have remained strong in not contacting him at all. You took your latest split like a pro, and tried your best to make him believe you don't need him or miss him at all).

However, a broken engagement is ten times worse than your average breakup. Therefore, what Blake doesn't know is that you cry about him every night and that you're popping far too many chocolates these days. Your lack of coherency though paints a completely different picture than the current reality. The anesthesia insists that you should text him and tell him EXACTLY how you feel about him, and how excited you are for your upcoming nuptials (which are most definitely canceled). Despite the reality of everything, you really truly believe that you and

Blake got back together. Perhaps it's because you still dream about it all the time? Your loopy ways have convinced you that you are a pair again, and that he wants you to text him and inform him that you are out of surgery…and of course, to remind him of your everlasting love for him.

All you can think about is getting your phone back. Maybe there's a reason other than the obvious that we have someone else hold our phones during the surgery/recovery process? As soon as you reunite with your parents, they realize they are going to have quite a care for a while. You're so bruised under the eyes that you look like Miss Piggy… if she lost a bar fight. No matter your condition or the state of your appearance, you want to text Blake and NOW!

You grab your phone and ignore all the nurse's instructions, mumble a few things to your daddy which makes zero sense, and try to lean over your wheelchair (any and all leaning over is against the rules for six weeks). You are clearly one of those reckless out of control patients who thinks they can run a marathon afterwards. The nurse cautions your parents to keep a close eye on you, because you're a strong one, and the fact that you sat right up after surgery indicates that you are going to try to do too much…which could obviously hinder the recovery process. Mom is listening attentively to the nurse's instructions while Dad's job is to make sure you don't hurt yourself.

In your phone, you are hyperactively looking for the name "Blake," forgetting that you changed his name to "Mr. Insensitive." You decide to check out that "Mr. Insensitive" contact under your one touch list wondering who the heck it is. You realize its Blake's number listed under the mysterious entry. You have zero recollection of ever editing him in such a way.

"Daddy, why'd you change Blake's name in my phone when I was in surgery," you ask.

"I didn't touch a thing," insists Dad. "I'm pretty sure that is what you put his name in there as after you two broke up," he added.

"DAD! We did not break up! Stop making things up, please. It's really upsetting me. He just asked me to marry him. Blake and I love each other. I would never ever call him such a thing," you say with your eyes open a mile wide.

After Mom gets done talking to the nurse, she agrees with your Dad.

"Sweetie, you told me last night that you are done with Blake and over him. You said you wouldn't text him even if you were paid to. You even told me to make sure that you don't have a weak moment, and that if you do…to stop you no matter what," says Mom.

"I did not! Why are you guys making up stuff?" you ask again.

Mom then tells you to send Lauryn a quick text to let her know how you're feeling.

"Out suregry. I am well.nose is betiful," you text her.

"Glad to hear it sis. Get some rest. Love you Leah," she replies.

Then you type your message for Mr. Insensitive…of course.

"Suregery did ☺ Waant2 cu now.missuU so mcuh finance.Nose b prety for or wedding!!! Hapyy we bAck togtr.I luv yu more babeypie☺ ☺"

Thirty seconds later, you get a message that reads, "Huh!? Are you okay? What is going on?"

You reply with, "yESSS babypie.cant wiat formy. Flowers.cantkiiss for fewdays tho ☹"

After sending him a few more messages expressing your delusional excitement about seeing him and him replying in confusion…you FINALLY come to grips with what you did.

"Oh no!" you cry.

"What!?" asks Mom.

"I texted Blake messages about loving him, missing him, and getting married. I forgot we broke up," you reply.

"Oh no," says Mom. "Honey, you're not supposed to be talking at all. Just hand me your phone."

As your mom begins to read your message out loud, she and your dad rotate from "Oh no's" to laughter (though they are trying to pretend that they don't find the situation the least bit humorous since you are clearly upset).

"Please text him back and tell him I didn't mean any of that, Mom! Please help me with this mess. My face hurts and Blake knows I still want him. I feel the worst," you say with tears rolling down your cheeks.

"Honey, please don't cry. You're getting your cast wet, and you need to be careful with your face," she says.

Mommy dearest decides to try her best to bail you out.

"Blake, this is Leah's mom. She just had a very major surgery, and she wants to apologize for the mix-up. She was feeling very out of it and confused. She says to tell you that she is happy and she wishes you the best."

Mom gets the classic "K" reply. You arrive home, and obviously there are zero flowers in sight. If this were the movies though, there'd be rose petals spread everywhere…but it's not the movies. This isn't the movie "Serendipity," nor is it "Bed of Roses." Blake isn't going to "get it"…he isn't going to make things right. You are going to have to recover without him and deal with the fact that you poured your sappy heart out to him. You take one look in the mirror at your hideous sight and begin to cry again.

Six weeks later, you and "Mr. Insensitive" return to your complete and utter dysfunction, before breaking up all over again. Next time you go under anesthesia…because with you, there WILL be a next time… you are going to leave your phone HOME. After all, why does a non-driving, loopy patient need one following a surgery anyways? Lesson learned! Maybe?….maybe not!

Harsh Leah Reality #26: Extended Family Get-together Woes

Scenario #1: Maybe it's time for another family reunion at your hometown park…oh joy! You love this time of year like you loved your last kidney stone. Everyone is ooing and awing over each other's baby bumps. By the way, who made up the term "baby bump" anyways? Wouldn't it be nice if that new pop culture term could just bump its way out of existence? No one bothers to ask you about your career or anything. Let's be real here…if you're not married with three kids by your age…you're simply not accomplished in any way, shape, or form, right? Right. How dare you be different?

You're the outcast of the room, and you know it. You officially feel like Toula prior to her "Big Fat Greek Wedding." Who really cares if you worked hard, found strength in your independence, and accomplished your wildest dreams, and then some? You can't talk child rearing, you can't talk PTA, you can't talk soccer, and you can't talk gardening. You really have nothing to contribute. Not to mention, you are also going to die alone, right? You figure you better treat your young relatives well, for one of them will be booking your nursing home one day. One of them will be bringing you fluffy slippers and floral flannel pajamas someday.

As you awkwardly look for a seat you realize pretty much every table is full of couples and or families. You take your plate of comfort food over to the table of teens to their mid-20's.

"Well, I guess I'll have a seat at the single's table you say," (to everyone who is younger than you).

"Suit yourself…I have a girlfriend. She just couldn't make it today. Leah, seriously, do you have Alzheimer's or what?" your little brother asks.

After realizing you are the singlemost, singlest person at your table, you realize the only true single is the toddler table. Well maybe not, because your four-year-old cousin Ella said she's got herself a boyfriend at preschool.

Ahh…"Just another day in paradise!"

Scenario #2: Or…maybe it's time for you to attend another family Christmas (husbandless and childless of course). You're about as excited for yet another extended family get together as you were for your root canal. There's going to be a great big potluck in which Aunt Glinda just always has to pinch your cheeks and call you out on your boxed or "slice and bake" recipe.

She will always say something to the effect of, "I spose when you getcha a man, you'll feel the need to become a little more domesticated, and just maybe you'll try some of those recipes I've given you."

Then there's your cousin Jill who just cannot help but show off the blinding glow coming from her left hand to confirm that her millionaire CEO love just proposed last week. Oh yes, and then there's cousin Angie, who is two years younger than you. She's getting out of her minivan with her four perfect children and her perfect husband. She's staying home while Mr. Perfect works and provides all that she wants, needs and more. She just wanted to announce today that they are expecting their fifth child! She figured they might as well have their children all close in age while they're still young. It's amazing to her and apparently everyone else in the room that you haven't even begun!

You were kind of secretly hoping that everyone would focus all their attention on Jill and Angie, rather than turn their attention to your assumed "loneliness." Now that you are in the spotlight, you are slightly irritated.

Before you know it, you've heard everything from "You really need a good man."...

To..."Women shouldn't have to be alone and work so hard."...

To "I had no idea that you and Blake broke up last year?"

To "Aren't you about to be 29 or is it like 32?...time is wasting away,"

AND...your favorite: "So tell me what you're REALLY doing with your life? Haven't you "made it" in the industry, yet? When are you going to give up, grow up, and move back home?" (Sigh...if only they understood what you HAVE accomplished and the odds you had to beat to get there).

Oh yes...and then there is..."You're just too picky!"

"You can't have it all!"

"If you keep this up, you will be single for the rest of your life."

"If you're waiting on someone perfect, you won't find it!"

"Life isn't a fairy tale!"

"You do know you can't just have babies forever, dontcha?.." chimes in Aunt Glinda.

"Yes, Aunt Glinda. I'm aware," you politely respond.

However, what you really want to say is, "Why, NO Aunt Glinda! I didn't pay attention in Anatomy class. I also don't have a shred of common sense either! I thought it might be cool to become a mother while everyone else my age is becoming a grandmother…just to be different, ya know!? I'm a leader…not a follower!"

Oh wait, in this case…that would be considered following wayyyyy behind. Trailing wayyyy off into the distance, but that's okay! Maybe you can be a trend-setter for younger women.

The Auntie lectures don't stop there though.

"If you would stop wasting your time on that loser who isn't giving you the time of day, you would see that someone else is willing to treat you much better."

"That man right there would definitely provide for you and take good care of you," she says pointing at Billy Bob Tanner, the family friend who is still single at 46 years old.

Seriously? The day you marry Billy Bob Tanner would be the day that all of hades freezes over.

If you're anything like Leah, you've probably heard at least one, if not all of these throughout your lifetime. People will try to convince you that you need to lighten up and perhaps you do to some extent… but perhaps, you don't.

Harsh Leah Reality #27: Dancing with Your Arch Nemesis

On your new path of self-improvement, you decide to develop and journal a fierce new health and fitness routine, which consists of working out five days a week and changing your eating habits. You figure if you get rock hard abs and bulging muscles, you cannot only feel better about yourself, but you can also drop kick the next man who breaks your heart. Just kidding. Or are you? Okay, so maybe you won't act on your emotions, but it certainly is fun to entertain the thought.

Anyways, this new pledge isn't just a temporary phase that will be soon forgotten. It is a lifestyle change, except for the occasional nights in which you must pop in the chick flick with a completely unrealistic far-fetched ending, and cry over a gallon of Rocky Road ice cream. Except for those cheat nights, there will be no more midnight munchies, triple thick milkshakes, onion rings, or Funfetti cupcakes for a while. Basically, if it's amazing and satisfies your appetite, you won't be eating it. If it is tasteless, bland, and leaves your tummy begging for more, it is on your new daily menu, and you can intake a whole 1,500 calories of it.

However, you cannot see the desired results unless you put in the necessary cardio, strength trainings, and of course join the new Zumba class that your friend has been pushing you to attend. You doubt your ability to not look like a complete fool in such a class, but decide, "why not?"

You go to class one without buying any new outfits. You're still wearing your same tacky, faded, high school workout gear that you wore 14 years before. You tell yourself it is a workout, in which you're just going to sweat and look grimy by the end of the night anyways. With that in mind, you also throw your hair back into the worst looking mess you've ever seen and decide makeup is also pointless, as is covering up that massive zit that looks like a third eye. You will worry about cuteness later, and if you put enough into this workout to deserve the reward of spending your money on adorable workout clothes, you may consider styling it up then.

For now, you're pumped, you're motivated, you're focused…and you're SHOCKED to see your ex-boyfriend's new fiancé Dramatic Drusilla walk through the door. What doesn't surprise you is that she has her equally evil sidekick Annoying Anastasia with her. They immediately give you the stare down as if they own the place, and you're not allowed to be there or something, and then proceed to quite obviously whisper about you. While they're not looking, you find yourself giving the dirtiest looks you've ever given behind anyone's unknowing backs. It's amazing that they're still hung up on the fact that you briefly dated her ex-boyfriend years before. It reminds you of preschool story hour that you used to have with them. They weren't your friends then, and they most certainly aren't now. Yes, you knew these girls from childhood. They randomly end up in the city you're living in out of all the places in the world, and Drusilla randomly ends up dating your ex (who is NOT from back home this time). Now, they're randomly at your Zumba class. You can hear "it's a small world after all" playing in your head over and over again.

Even though it was YOU who dumped her new man of the hour before he and her even knew each other, and your chemistry was beyond weak, and you used to sometimes even dread his sloppy kisses, Drusilla hasn't forgotten about you or trying to ruin your life. Not to mention you've had several relationships since...ones that actually broke your heart. Still though, the idea of Drusilla being engaged to him is more than a little irritating, and the fact that she openly has a problem with you fuels your fire even more. Just as you figured Drusilla and Anastasia would, they grew up to be the catty sand-paper irritants that you expected, and now here they are at your Zumba class giving you the watchdog eye.

However, you're NOT about to let them stop you from getting in shape, and you're certainly not going to let them intimidate you. No, you're not! If anything, this will cause you to work even harder than ever before. Not to mention, next time you see them, you will have on those cute, little, wallet-damaging, Victoria's Secret yoga shorts. You will also be boasting perfectly applied makeup and hair that looks like it should be featured in a shampoo commercial. You may get sweaty, but you are determined to be a hot mess...quite literally. Yes, you will, and you're going to out dance them, and make them want to stay far away from Zumba class. All you can hear is Patrick Swayze saying, "Nobody puts baby in a corner."

However, you're a bit nervous as you've NEVER done Zumba before, and you certainly were not a dancer in high school. You're probably going to look like you SHOULD be put in a corner. If you're being real with yourself, you can flat out admit that you actually cannot dance even if your life depended upon it. Your parents didn't pay for ballet lessons like Drusilla's mommy and daddy did for her. On top of that, your sinus infection and "hack up a lung" respiratory inflammation is getting to you, and you can't breathe out of either nostril. Heck, you barely can even breathe through your mouth, but you're just going to have to suck it up and show it up. After all, excuses aren't allowed in workouts…even if you do feel like you need to be transported to the ER ASAP!

The music starts, and the instructor begins at a rapid pace of what you swear must be at least 50 mph while throwing her head, arms, hands, thighs, booty, and body parts you forget you even have, into places you didn't think possible. She is clearly a professional, you are clearly an amateur, and you are clearly NOT in a beginning Zumba class, but an advanced one to put it mildly. Trying to mimic your incredibly skillful instructor, you begin pushing yourself beyond your capacity, acting as if you've been participating in this class your whole life. You are hoping that if you pretend you know what you are doing, the instructor, along with Drusilla and Anastasia, will be fooled by it as well. Your body seems to be aching after five minutes, which you didn't think was possible, and you already need an inhaler, which you've never ever used, but you're not slowing up. You refuse to let your arch nemesis win.

You can see the evil twin sisters still eyeing you, but not for long. Ahhhh…they are out the door within five minutes. Sigh…you always knew you would get your fulfilling showdown with Drusilla. Hope that her man doesn't mind the fact that she's going to be "more to love" after she quits her other seasonal so-called workout routines. So much for her New Year's resolution. After she exits, you find yourself slowing way down and returning to a human Jello-like state. By the time class is over and you've nearly convinced yourself that you will not be back ever again, you think of Drusilla's snotty face…and then get in the car and take your deserving self, shopping!…at Victoria's Secret of course!

Harsh Leah Reality #28: The Broken Record of Bad Valentine's Days

Just the mention of this holiday makes you want to run for the hills. Instead of just a plain and simple day of no roses, no candy hearts, no kisses, and no loving…you've been getting slapped with insult to injury every single year. The day can't just be a simple annoyance! No, it's got to kick your butt…with a steel-toed work boot. Yes, you have had seven years of bad luck with this mushy gushy holiday. No, really. It's not a lie. It's a sad truth in your loveless life. What you're most terrified of is not necessarily being without a valentine yet again, but more so, having another really, really bad Valentine's Day. You are terrified of year eight also containing something non-traditional and extra cruel. If the seven years of bad luck is really true, then that means year eight should be better, right? Hmm, there wasn't any mirror breaking in this case, but you've just got to assume that the curse should be broken this year. Well, it isn't looking so good, Sista. Sorry about your luck. You have officially decided that if this cycle really does continue into year eight, that this isn't just the seven years of bad luck…but in fact, a life-long curse.

When did things head so south, and cause you to write up a mission of boycotting Heart Day? The story is somewhat similar to "How the Grinch stole Christmas." Yes, every Grinch has their reason for their heart turning so cold to any given holiday. You were like the young Grinch seven years ago. You believed in the holiday and wanted to be an active participant, but you got burnt badly, and your heart shrunk by three sizes that day. Something terrible happened to you on that very day, and it just continued…year after year. Like the Grinch, you now make it your mission to personally protest the holiday. You want to clear the store shelves of all candy and cards, and the florists of all their flowers. Okay, but seriously..

Your issues with the lover's holiday all started seven years ago when you actually had a boyfriend, and you were in a committed relationship that seemed like it could be on its way to the altar. You were just 24, and at that point and time in your life, you actually knew what it was like to have a sweetheart. Your Valentine's the previous year was great. It included a gigantic life-sized card from this same boyfriend, sweet gifts, a nice dinner, a movie, and the typical kind of Valentine's Day that any love-struck girl might expect.

So, now, we start from the beginning of the agonizing journey: On this particular day seven years ago, your college boyfriend Dillon surprised you with tickets to a special Valentine's Day cruise. You were so unbelievably excited to embark on the adventure that you couldn't even believe it. What you didn't know was that night would be the beginning of a long line of cruel and unusual punishments for years to come. Before your date that night, you felt a sickness overcoming you. You didn't want to tell Dillon how incredibly horrible you felt, because he had put so much money into this special present for you. It was supposed to be such a romantic night. What could've been more romantic than a cruise with your better half? Well, when you feel like you're on your death bed…anything would be more romantic than being out in the cold in a public place, on a ship that you cannot escape.

It was as if you felt the winds of change in the air that night as you stood on the boat deck wondering what could possibly be wrong with you. Somehow you knew that things were going downhill from that moment on. You couldn't socialize with other people on the boat, your throat felt like you swallowed a sword, and you shivered uncontrollably feeling like you needed to be in a warm bed. You can recall feeling the sickest you have ever felt. You can remember leaving your boyfriend for a bathroom break, and losing your whole entire dinner that you could barely eat to begin with. You rotated from cold chills to sweats, and felt like you could faint.

Somehow you survived the cruise, but by the next morning, you realized that the winds of change had followed you home. You had taken a strep culture the day before. The clinic called to confirm that you had strep AND the flu, and there you were also on your vicious monthly cycle with indescribable pains. For three days straight, you stayed in bed, seriously wondering if you might be dying. Dillon was still there for you. Surprisingly, he actually emerged from his video game playing for a few minutes. He brought you lots of Vitamin C and TLC…or at least you think he did. (You pretty drugged up and sometimes people dream strange things when they're sick). However, something in you knew that you and Dillon were on the outs too. You were right.

Two months later, you and Dillon, your "almost fiancé" parted ways after you caught him cheating..

A year later when Red Day rolled around, you were leaving your college internship in your yucky khakis. Oh, it's so glamorous when the Mom of an ex-boyfriend you dated when you were 18 years old randomly calls you (texting did not exist in those days), and asks you to join her for dinner while her hubby is away on a business trip. Pam had been like a second mother to you, and she just happened to be in town…so you didn't think too much of it. You knew ahead of time that Valentine's Day with the ex's mother could potentially be a little awkward, but you still adored her. Besides, a good meal sounded nice since you didn't have anyone else to be out with that night. You met her out at Olive Garden. What you didn't realize was that she was bringing her other son "Lee" along. One bite into your breadstick, you realized that Pam was trying to set you up with Lee. Yes, she had liked you so well that when it didn't work with Liam, she instead decided that you and Lee would be better together. Sweet? Maybe. A good idea? Not hardly.

After putting that painfully awkward Valentine's Day behind you and chalking it up as one that gave you a good laugh, the next year seemed to roll around even quicker. Yes, the more your love life fell apart, the faster the clock seemed to move. Hoping that "third times a charm" would hold true since you had just endured two rough February 14's, you were remaining optimistic. You had just started your first real professional job, and though you were undoubtedly single, you weren't TOO affected by your solo-ness just yet. You were trying to begin life on your own, and you just simply weren't ready to focus on all that marriage stuff.

The night before Valentine's Day, Donnie, a fellow business partner, phoned you about having dinner with him. You had heard rumors that

Donnie wanted more than a business relationship with you, but you had kind of shrugged them off. Besides, Donnie just wanted to go over some "ideas" for an upcoming project, and hey, why not? You had nowhere else to be. It was so very obvious that you hadn't learned your lesson from the year before, yet you failed to make the connection between everything. Donnie insisted that he come pick you up, but your natural blondeness still didn't catch on. You let him pick you up assuming you were going to go to a middle of the road kind of restaurant. No, he chose the priciest restaurant in the whole entire city.

You were taking your first sip of your lemon water, when Donnie said, "Leah…there's something I've got to tell you…"

"Yes, Donnie? You don't think my idea is good enough? I realize I might be missing the mark. I'm open to suggestions."

"Leah, I'm crazy about you. It's more than just a crush. From the second I laid eyes on you, I fell for you…head over heels. I know it is real love. In fact, I know for sure you're the woman I want to spend the rest of my life with. I didn't plan on proposing tonight, but if you'd say "yes" right now, then I would gladly propose…because you would make me the happiest man alive," Donnie expressed.

For a minute, you honestly thought he might be joking, but as he had shared his "feelings," a wild look had come across his eyes.

"Donnie, are you serious?" you asked.

"Serious as I've ever been. Leah, I love you…so, so much. I already think about naming our children, and where we're going to live," he gushed.

He then proceeded to present you with a book of poems – a daily poem for every day he had known you for these past three months.

"Leah, Valentine's Day makes exactly three months of knowing you. It's so obvious that we're meant to b…"

"Donnie, I am so sorry for this, but I do not feel the same way about you that you feel about me. I see you as my friend and business partner. I don't want to be anything other than professional with you. This is all sweet, but frankly, I can't give you want you want. You're going to make some other girl so happy someday." (Admittedly, in your mind, you were really thinking, or "creeped out" is more like it).

Then came the tears…crocodile tears. You weren't expecting it to go that far, but oh it did. You had made a grown man cry in a public restaurant. At that moment, you suggested that he head on home, and that you call a friend to pick you up. Unfortunately, he still insisted on driving you home. You tried to talk him out of it, but then it occurred to you that ALL your other friends were out on a date…because after all, it was V-Day. You were stuck with "Mr. Way Too Deep," and there wasn't any getting around it.

You insisted that you weren't hungry anyways, and he said he wasn't either…after you crushed his heart. As the two of you drove away, his uncontrollable sobbing continued. He begged you to reconsider his offer. He spent the entire drive trying to sell himself to you.

It was the most agonizing 20 minutes of your life. You felt mean, selfish, flattered, completely appalled and creeped out all at once. Had this been the worst Valentine's yet? Close to it at least.

Year four, you had just ended things with good ole' Joe Limburtony after you caught him cheating on you…red-handed. You knew he was ridiculously dishonest with you, but you weren't about to let that ruin your day. You phoned your friend Hillary for a night out on the town, which included formal attire and an expensive dinner at that fancy restaurant that you can't ever afford (NOT the one from year three. You were in need of a clean slate). After ordering your sirloin and overloaded baked potato…your appetite left you immediately. You noticed two familiar faces being seated in the booth behind you: Joe and your so-called friend "Cami" (who had recently broken off her engagement). You tried to hold your composure…you really did, but you just couldn't. After burying your head in your hands, praying for the check to come prematurely, you began asking yourself, "WHY ME?" Hillary nudged the server and told him what was going on, and suggested that you get boxes to go. Not only did Mr. Server come back with boxes to go, but he returned with a complimentary chocolate rose for you to remember your experience by. Aw, how sweet!

As you were getting up to leave, Joe had the nerve to say "Wait!?... Leah! How are you?"

"Oh just beautiful," you replied with your eyes rotating from him to Cami.

"Actually Hillary and I have another place to be, so were outta here."

As you made your way to the car, you knew that you didn't have anywhere to be, but on your couch crying. As you were driving, you were Facebooking it, and deleting both Cami and Joe, while Hillary tried to warn you to watch for oncoming cars. She tried to assure you that you could do so much better. You didn't believe her. You were officially going to die an old, lonely maid.

Would year five of this craziness bring you a different fortune? Not likely, but you decided you weren't even taking a chance. You instead planned to get on an airplane and spend that V-Day with family. You decided that if you left town, MAYBE you would stand a chance at having a somewhat "uneventful" day. Not likely, because the man on your mind would follow you home…mentally. You had a dysfunctional relationship of sorts with Blake, whom you had met a couple years before (yes, him again), but you had no idea what to make of it. At that time in your life, you had fallen harder for him than you had for anyone else, but your track record was really beginning to scare you. It also didn't help that he kept going back and forth with his ex-girlfriend.

Before you head to your home state of Kentucky for a getaway, Blake came over to swoon you, and to provide you with unrealistic hope for your unrealistic future together. For the first time ever, you and Blake left the friend zone after the last couple years of flirting with the relationship zone. Fact or fiction, reality or fairy-tale…you were completely taken up with his words. In fact, you were so taken up with his words, that a part of you was even asking yourself why you were going to Kentucky for this special day, when you could instead be spending it with him.

Nonetheless, you were not about to cancel your flight. You made a decision to spend this time with family, and that is what you would be standing by.

When you arrived in Kentucky, your Mama played the "20 questions about Blake game." You were batting your eyelashes and blushing as you gushingly answered each and every one. You were in love. You didn't truly know what love was until Blake, but now that you did, you knew it was a feeling that you wanted to hold onto forever. The two of you exchanged some texts during your visit home, but deep within your gut, you found yourself fearing that things were about to fall apart. You knew it when you stepped out into that extreme cold front that had struck in Kentucky. The cold winter wind made you believe that an avalanche was heading your way.

As you were attempting to ignore your disturbing feelings, you were talking with your Mom over some Valentine's Day peanut M & M's. As you were about to pop the 83rd one into your mouth, you stopped and realized something was extra special about that one. Could it be the shape of a…heart? Woah! Yes! Okay, so maybe you should rid yourself of those negative thoughts? Maybe this was a sign! A sign that "love is here" and that you will be a Mrs. at that time next year…or maybe not…

You did send your unique heart-shaped M & M onto Mar's chocolate with a photo of you and your rare find. You did get a response and a letter declaring that they enjoyed your picture. You also got the assurance that it had been displayed on their bulletin board, fascinating all who stopped to take a glance at it.

However, the heart-shaped M & M was not a sign of a better year. When you flew back into town, it was not Blake who picked you up. It was your loyal guy friend Steve instead. You found out via Facebook that Blake had gone back to his ex-girlfriend. Yes, the very girl who he had complained soooo much about just happened to win him back! Of course it didn't last long though.

You and Blake did end up talking three months later, but nothing was resolved. Instead the dysfunctional on-again off-again relationship continued until the fall.

Year six, you finally found yourself with a Valentine just months before Valentine's Day, but would the two of you make it to lover's day?

Close, but he decided to break up with you the night before its official arrival. You knew he was struggling for money, but you didn't know he was that *cowardly*.

The worst part? He said, "I'm sorry…I know you said you always have a bad Valentine's Day, and I know I just made it worse."

The next day? You were surrounded at work with flowers, chocolates, and cards being delivered to the office…none for you, of course.

Year seven, you finally convinced yourself that you had beaten the curse, because you actually had someone ON the day of Valentine's Day. Well, you thought at least. You weren't Facebook official or anything, but as far as you knew, you two were supposed to be monogamous, exclusive, or whatever it is that they call it these days. You weren't completely sure how you felt about him yet, but you were thankful to have him. However, it was a long distance relationship. Ken in Kentucky was your childhood crush back in your home state, and you two were acting just like a couple…therefore, you were…you thought? Despite your confusion of your title, you decided to do something simple, but very special for him. You put together a collage of your favorite photos over the last several months, and included a special note. You were careful not to be overly mushy or to even so much as use the word "love," but you wanted him to know that he was appreciated and cared for. After having serious technical issues at the photo booth, you had his gift made…two hours later. You then mailed him that picture with a magnet frame that you were just so proud of.

Strangely, a very weird illness had overcome you for the past week. What is it with you and strange illnesses on V-Day? Was this a flashback to the beginning of your hatred for Heart Day? Maybe since this was how the curse began, this was also how it would end?

Among your many symptoms, every time you ate ANY food, your face would swell up. You have a long history of ear, nose, and throat (ENT) problems, but this odd acting illness had even fooled your regular doctor. As you approached V-Day and walked into the ENT office with your issues, you found out that you were dealing with something fairly urgent that needed surgery right away. Okay, so no huge fights, breakups, dinner with an ex's mom, or super awkward moments on V-Day that year, but you found out that you needed surgery again. Okay, so surgery isn't fun, but surely Ken would have something waiting for you in the mailbox, right? Wrong!

He did call you later that night to thank you for getting him something, before saying, "I feel bad for not getting you anything in return. I know you've always had bad Valentine's Day, so I should have sent you something."

You're sitting there thinking, "It's not about the gifts, but it is about showing I'm cared about, and since you KNEW this was a rough holiday for me, why in the world would you not so much as even send me a card?"

You ended up having your friend Hillary over to watch a movie with you. Your movie of choice could have been classified as anything but a chick flick.

The night ended with Ken asking, "So how was your Valentine's Day?"
You told him, "Good."

However, what you really wanted to say was, "Other than finding out I'm very sick and have to have an urgent surgery, and didn't even receive so much as a Hallmark from you…I'm still kicking, buddy!"

You tried to assure yourself that Ken would make up for this obvious shortcoming in the upcoming weeks, but you soon found out, you had the bar set way too high for him. He didn't acknowledge you then, or on any holiday ever again. Yep…apparently you were never an official couple, and he never wanted a relationship. Whatever it was…you two were history two months later. As a little girl the name Ken was so dreamy and so perfect – all because of your handsome Mattel doll. You imagined Ken to be the quintessential man, but this real life Ken didn't treat you even close to the way that you had your Ken treat your Barbie. This Ken officially destroyed your childhood, and your belief in gentlemen.

With all your combined history, no wonder you've become a Valentine's Day Grinch. Secretly, you wish someone would come along, put the light back in your eyes, and a smile on your sneering face. Yes, you wish that someone would cause your heart to grow three sizes again…Okay, let's not get cheesy here. You're fine single…just fine.

Harsh Leah Reality #29: The "F" word

Oh, by the way, out of all the words you hear associated with "love" or whatever it is that you call it these days…the "F" word is the worst. Really, how many freakin times does a guy have to say the "F" word? Welcome to modern-day America in which the term "friend" is used more loosely than a stripper.

"We're really, really, really, really good friends…"

Really, how many times do you really have to say "really" before we're really "more than friends?"

You have decided that you must "beware" if you hear a man call a woman his "friend" these days. A friend could in fact actually hold true to its actual meaning of they truly are platonic, or he could in fact be practicing baby-making with that chick every night. Either way, she may still have the title of "friend."

You have harsh memories of the dreaded "F" word which often replay in your mind. You can recall the love of your life ending things by saying, "I mean what would be so wrong with us being friends? Friends are a really good thing to have!"

Are you supposed to do a backflip over the fact that he wants to be friends…oh and temporary, distant friends at that? You know how it goes. You can't stay friends forever. Either he'll get married or you will, and then your artificial friendship will be over. Oh wait, you don't have to worry about YOU getting married, but you know he will…and then yeah, you'll have nothing. It's a curse word and it drives a female crazy. Just leave a girl. Do whatever you want…just don't say the freakin "F" word.

Your exes all seem to think that you need to add another "friend" to the roster: A friend who they don't want to remain "platonic" with of course. I mean really, what makes these guys think that you want to hear the "F" word following a breakup?

Since you hate THE "F" word unless someone is your "actual friend," you decided to beat Ken to the punch when you could see your relationship was a plane that was never going to leave the tarmac. Yes, Ken – the guy who strung you along without any good reason. He just wasn't committing and you called him on it as he was taking you back to the airport (hence that's why you were thinking with airplane analogies). Go figure…just like the movies. Except this guy isn't about to realize his mistake. No, he isn't going to chase the plane, and he isn't going to interrupt the flight. As you're in the middle of breaking up your "whatever it was" relationship, you say…

"Oh and by the way…don't you dare ask me to be friends, because I don't want to hear it…you know why?…Because I have enough freakin friends, okay!? I have enough friends for 365 days of the year, and I don't need you. This is done…you're cut off. Now leave me alone."

As he drops you off at the airport, your scene doesn't look anything like Hollywood…not even a little. This isn't "The Wedding Singer" and this isn't "Love Actually." This is real life here. You angrily grab your bags out of the back of his car while he asks "if you can still talk,"… which is a unique way of him not using the "F" word yet still asking the same dreaded question.

You even surprise yourself with your sudden sass as you say… "Um NO!"

And you STORM off in those stilettos you should've never worn.

It's going to be a long walk with that 80 pound suitcase from the weekend you should've never had…but you're not about to let him see you struggle. You're only letting him believe that you're a spitfire in stilettos. You are independent, you are strong…to his face at least.

Harsh Leah Reality #30: The Reoccurring Breakup Drill

You're not exactly sure if it's funny, angering, or just plain sad, how used to moving on you are. Perhaps all three. You know the drill: You barely slept all night and you feel like death (though death has become a familiar feeling). You contemplate staying in bed, but remind yourself that you've got to face the world eventually, so you might as well do it now.

You say "This is the day the Lord has made…let us rejoice and be glad in it,"…but sadly you're not feeling glad about getting up, your latest split, or facing the day just yet. Sulking is such a tempting option.

You throw on those dress pants in which the waist keeps expanding. They're sagging and trying their best to show off your leopard panties, and make you look more like an aspiring rapper than a business woman. You listen to a combination of upbeat and heart-wrenching songs on the way to work, and think "yeah right," or "yeah I'll never recover like the song implies." You didn't have much time for makeup, but you do arrive at the office 5 minutes early, so you can paint on a little bit of a face…both metaphorically and literally. You're pretty sure that your already messy pony tail becomes messier as your life becomes messier, but at least you're there and at least you're working like a boss.

You sip that coffee you swore you were going to stop drinking. Then you realize the energy the coffee's caffeine provides you with is about the length of your latest relationship. You can barely stomach your lunch, but your friend assures you that you've got to eat, and this too shall pass. You replay the unfortunate heartbreak for the thousandth time while she assures you that the right one is out there, and that this one didn't deserve you.

You tell her you're done for good as she points out good looking guys at lunch and you tell her, "But he's just not Ken…he's just not…no one is…and no one will ever be again. Well, except maybe Blake, but we all know him and I just don't work…and honestly, I don't know why I ever even want him. He makes me unhappy most of the time. It's Boy Next

Door who has always made me the happiest and brought out the best in me, but him and I just go in circles. My life is just one big circle.."

You check your Facebook only to see that you have a message from "Needy Nelson" asking you out for coffee…for the 50th time. Sigh, when will this poor guy ever take the hint? Why can't you have a notification from the guy you actually want? As you're carrying on and on about the indescribable pain you're enduring, your exes are texting you and interrupting your hour of head-clearing.

When you get back from lunch, you realize it's time to reevaluate your picture décor in your cubicle. Sigh…your cubicle looks pathetic compared to almost everyone else's as it is, and now you have to strip it down even more. Your picture with "loser boy" has got to go ASAP.

Your friends have bright, happy spaces full of pictures of their spouses and children…and you have…pictures of your dog. Your favorite man besides your Daddy is your dog "Nash" of course. Within Suzie's 10X10 space of photos she has Jaden's first lost tooth, Maddie's potty training, Bryson riding without training wheels, and pretty much every other detail of her children's lives since birth. You on the other hand, have pictures of Nash's first night home, Nash's first birthday, Nash's obedience school graduation, and Nash's first rodent kill. Of course in the mixture, is a picture of your family (the one you were born into), and your girlfriends (who are all either engaged or married).

Sigh…oh well. Now that you and loser boy broke up, you have to put away his face. What do you do? You put his picture in the back of the frame behind your other exes. Yes, you just keep putting your latest ex behind an earlier ex.

Then you ask yourself, "Why did I even bother putting him up?"

Since this frame has displayed multiple photos of other failed relationships, you ask yourself: "Is this frame cursed, is my love life cursed, or both?"

Yes, this very frame is soo full of exes being covered up that it can barely hide it anymore. It occurs to you that during your time in this position, you've experienced five breakups of some sort. You got your heart broken, but you broke hearts in return. Hmmmm…either you need to stop dating, or you've been in this position five years too long. Perhaps both. Still, you replace the front picture with a super old picture of you and your sister. She looks like she's twelve in the picture, and she would likely kill you for using that one if she ever would happen to make her way to your workspace.

After giving your cube a pathetic makeover, someone comes over and points to the family picture and asks if brother is your boyfriend. Sigh…..

As the day continues, you get the "you've lost weight" comments. You tell everyone your new diet is really working for you —it really is, but you don't tell them its 5% healthy eating, 5% working out, mixed with 90% breakup blues.…

Harsh Leah Reality #31: Improper Table Etiquette & First Date Woes

The older you get, the more you reflect on the journey: "The Good, the Bad and the Ugly." You still remember all of your wonderful and all your horrible dates just like yesterday. Now, here you are about to add another memory. You thought you and your latest date were bonding over that over-priced spaghetti…you really did. You were so happy with yourself for not flinging it all over yourself. First date…white shirt… ordering spaghetti…it all seemed like a recipe for disaster. However, you were starting to have confidence in your dinner etiquette abilities. You talked, you laughed, and your prospect kept looking straight at your mouth.

"Ahhhhh…he must wanna kiss me," you thought.

Well, he didn't kiss you. He told you he had a nice time, but didn't try anything…at all. As you get into his car though, you still felt good about him, and assure yourself he just wants to take it slow. Then again, guys almost always kiss at the end of a date.

He has to run back inside the restaurant to get his jacket, and you have a whole 30 seconds to make sure every hair is still in place. You just cannot wipe off that dorky "I've got a crush" smile. You quickly take advantage of pulling down his car mirror.

"Maybe he'll kiss me when he walks me to my door," you wonder.

That makes him such a gentleman. The ideal guy would take things slow, right? Of course he would. As you reflect on the night, you recall that it was a night of vibrant color: The tablecloths were a deep magenta color. His eyes were blue, his shirt was black.........and so is the space between your two front teeth. Oh my gosh! We're not just talking about a piece of garlic here...we're talking about garlic on steroids. It is so big, and so lodged that your man of the hour probably thought it was a bug or something.

After 20 minutes of freaking out, you assure yourself this would be a really stupid reason for him not to give you another chance.

So much for those reassurance talks you do with yourself...You never hear from him again. It may or may not have been because of your garlic issue.

Oh well, that was far from being your only first date disaster. Your biggest dating disasters happened in your early 20's. There was the time you picked up your little queso cheese cup and it pretty much exploded...alllllllll over you. You're still not exactly sure how that was possible, but apparently it was, because it most certainly happened. Your date who you barely knew came flying across the table to help wipe off your dry clean only vintage leather jacket. If that wasn't bad enough, you ALSO wound up sitting in gum at some point that night.

As you were walking out of the movie theatre, your date informs you, "Uhhh, you've got something on the back of your pants. I think you sat in gum."

So there you were, trying to get to know this guy, and you were forced to become very quickly acquainted, as he was picking gum off your back side.

When you got back out to his car, you noticed the gum was on his leather seat.

Somehow, you ended up dating this particular guy a year and a half. You're not sure how...but you did. Maybe he was attracted to your clumsiness. That tough to remove gum even left a permanent spot on his seat, which remained when he traded off the car.

Not all of your first date disasters involve food though. You left the super long size sticker on the pair of those new jeans…and of course your date spotted it. You'll never forget the sore red eye from your new contacts date either. Then there were all those times that you had one strand of hair that just wouldn't curl for anything. All you could see when you looked in the mirror was that obnoxious straight piece. And that liquid eyeliner? It glides on beautifully until you're getting ready for a date. You go from a makeup artist to a three year old using their non-dominant hand.

With your first date history, you're always terrified to find out how much worse it can get…but with you, you always know it will probably get worse.

Harsh Leah Reality #32: Losing End of a Chick Flick Come True

Don't you just love it when you score tickets to watch that new chick flick on its first night in theatres? EVERYONE has been anticipating it, and you cannot wait to participate in the workplace discussions tomorrow.

It is a funny romantic comedy with an interesting storyline…you'll give it that. The plot is hilarious, and the scriptwriters are brilliant, though it is of course 95% predictable. You know how the story goes: It features five couples who get together during the course of the movie, have a break-up point in which they don't talk to each other, and in the end they all end up forgiving one another and everyone lives happily ever after, right? Right. Not to mention, the perfect proposal takes place and all the bystanders smile and clap. The makeup sessions happen in large crowds, in which the man is suddenly not afraid to pour his heart out in front of 200 people. He picks his lady up, spins her through the air, and their kiss lasts for what appears to be forever.

Uh huh...yep, you've seen it happen in real life. Okay, no you haven't. The probability of such a plot in real life is that maybe one or two of the five couples could work it back out, and even at that, there's no telling if it would last...but of course the credits roll with everything being perfect. It's a good thing they can't show you what happens after those credits roll, right? You would probably be pretty dang disappointed! Anyways, you enjoy the movie even though it was about as realistic as the pet unicorn you claimed you had as a child.

You wrap up your evening by going out to get some wings (notice they never really do that in the movies?) You of course pull out your iPhone, and try to be careful not to get hot sauce all over the screen, and then you jump onto none other than the life-controlling, drama-starting Facebook. At the top of the newsfeed is none other than your ex-boyfriend Ken's announcement of his engagement. His status was posted 41 minutes ago to be exact (since details of the exact time period of his big moment are crucial)! Sooo...that basically means while you were watching the unrealistic happy ending of the movie, your ex was realistically popping the question to his girl (whom he apparently found to be sooo much better than you), and evidently she said yes. He probably even proposed to her as the guy was proposing in the movie. Wouldn't that be sooooo cute if it were all nsync...fiction and reality all at once? Okay, maybe not.

Though you're definitely not devastated, you find yourself slightly annoyed and not exactly happy for them either. You were the good girlfriend, and you tried to do everything right, but it wasn't enough for him. However, you would now shoot him down faster than the speed of light if he were to come back your way. Heck, you're not sure why he's even your ex, as you're shocked you wanted him as a boyfriend in the first place. Still though, you're not exactly thrilled for him, and you certainly won't be writing a "Congratulations, I'm so happy for you," on his wall. You pride yourself in honesty, and it wouldn't be honest. Simple as that.

The chick flick characters got their happily ever after tonight and so did your ex…but you? You're on the losing end. Well, maybe not… wings = love.

Harsh Leah Reality #33: Independent…And You Like it That Way! Or Do You?

Okay…so maybe your older and younger sister were married by the time they were 22. In fact, pretty much all of your siblings were, or at least close to it. The middle child syndrome has contained so much awkwardness for you and so much extra stress for your poor parents. Not long after high school, they were happily gracing the doors of every bridal shop in town and beyond for your sisters. No sooner did they walk down the aisle before you found yourself hosting their baby showers. You're truly glad that everything has worked out so well for them, but as a result, it's made you very different than them.

Although strong women, they never really spent a day alone in their lives. They can't relate to your days of living all alone trying to make ends meet in a run down one bedroom apartment, in which your neighbors run a Meth lab. Your sisters went straight from mom and dad to their husbands. While life with their hubbies haven't been stress free, they've never really had to worry about their own oil changes, electronic trouble shooting, mysterious knocks on the door, constant encounters with creepers, and playing "fix it" woman. They probably also don't check behind their shower curtains for possible intruders every night they get home either.

But you my dear…have had to learn from personal experience that there isn't any intruder that could possibly defeat you, anything too heavy to lift, or any lid too tight for a woman living on her own. You see that gigantic spider in the shower? Yep, an independent woman probably needs to take care of that herself. Did you just see a creepy furry little creature with a long tail run across the floor? Yep, you probably better set a trap, because there isn't anyone else in the house who will be rescuing you from this disgusting rodent.

Remember that day your brakes randomly went out while you were driving? As usual, you called your poor Dad. After you got the car stopped and somehow managed to avoid a massive accident, you then had to take matters in your own hands. Thankfully, your guardian angel was with you, and you had a trusty dealership nearby that came to get you. However, unlike your sisters, you didn't have a husband to just run to your rescue, when your poor ole' master cylinder decided to say "good-bye." Your singleness is understandably giving your Dad fits. He wants you to find a man even more than you want to find a man.

You're just so used to being independent though that you're not sure you have room for anyone else. As time goes on, you are getting good at being alone. You do just fine carrying in those grocery bags by yourself and usually make it in one trip though you've cut off your circulation by the time you reach the top of the stairs! Not only that, but you toted and set up that brand new television, and put together that stand all by yourself. Your job may not be your dream job, but you're paying your bills on time or even early, and you do a great job of budgeting. You have your own little place which is the perfect size for a single person, and it's more than enough to keep clean. You have a life – plain and simple. You have Jesus, a great family, an incredible church, a group of trusty friends, and you know how to laugh…hard. You can make your own plans, stay up as late as you want, and spend your money however you want. You've discovered freedom and it's beautiful.. In fact, you're not sure if you ever want to give it up…ever again.

Except for having to call a maintenance man here and there…you are golden. You may not know exactly how to use each and every tool out there…but you have met a few tools in your lifetime…named Allen and Stanley. The last names Phillips, Black, and Decker have even been in your past at some point (pun intended)…

Harsh Leah Reality #34: Like Keith Whitley, You're No Stranger to the Rain

Ahh…why does rain have to be so symbolic? As you're walking out of the grocery store you see a bunch of women waiting near the exit. There is a torrential downpour going on outside, but you aren't going to stand around like a big baby. Unlike them apparently, you have places to be. Therefore, you are going to just have to tough it out because:

#1 You don't have a man to pick you up, and your car isn't going to magically start itself and come get you.

#2 You didn't bring an umbrella. Not that umbrellas are your friend anyways…but once again like Keith, you are however a friend of thunder. Your umbrellas usually are 'Gone with the Wind' (ah yes another chick flick), and they flip upside down, grab all the rain they can hold, and then drench you. So instead of looking like a wet rat, you end up looking like a drenched one.

You have no idea what it is like to have a man drive up and get you so you don't have to walk through the tsunami, but it's probably nice. Well, okay, your sweet dad who is one of the five good guys you know has always picked you and your mom up in the rain, but once again, he doesn't live here. Without hesitation, you walk past the crowd of big-eyed mamas that act like they're petrified of the 'mysterious water drops' coming from the sky. As you walk out into it like a boss, they look at you in utter amazement. What are you supposed to do? Wait there all night? The last time you checked, rain by itself has never killed anyone has it? (With the exception of the Wicked Witch of course).

Then it hits you. A profound meaningful thought actually enters your usually sharply sarcastic mind. You are fearless to the rain. The rain doesn't affect you in the way that it does them. In fact, you can't even feel the rain, because you have walked through it so many times. You are numb to it.

You once had a boss during your stint with door-to-door sales who told you that carrying an umbrella would only slow you down. Thus you went to the doors of strangers looking like you just jumped into the lake fully clothed. At least your drenched rat image kept any creepers from trying to come on to you. It was like a natural repellent. Who needs pepper spray when you have rain without an umbrella to uglify you to the repulsive point? With mascara rolling down your cheeks, you kept going for the day. You also didn't meet your quotas either.

In that moment, the most powerful analogy ever has become the representation of your journey. The longer one has walked through the rain, the less likely they are to fear it or to feel it. Rain is part of life for them. They are used to it. Thus, they become thicker skinned and have a lesser fear of storms. Maybe some of those other women haven't walked through the rain in the way that you have, and maybe a metaphorical hurricane is going to really shake those particular women up.

Then it hits you even harder. You survived a literal tornado in the worst part of town while standing outside because you had a FLAT TIRE. Surrounded by convicts in the ghetto during a tornado, without any means of transportation is definitely the ultimate survival. You're not just a survivor, girl...you're a dang warrior!

Harsh Leah Reality #35: Jealous of your neighbor/Life on the 3rd floor

You're a warrior except when it comes to getting up in the mornings. After hitting the snooze button at least ten times, you officially wake up for another magnificent Monday in the same ole fashion – (your pajamas are as unattractive as your attitude)...as are the random clothes you choose to put on. As usual, you're running a little late. Nonetheless, you take a minute to read your morning devotion which encourages you to begin each day with a new positive outlook. You really do believe in the importance of the good Lord's words...even though you continually struggle. Your devotion this morning just happens to be on "envy."

You almost walk out with two different shoes, but thankfully you catch yourself. The second you step out into the breezeway, you wonder if you are really living in the southern part of the United States of America…or if you are in fact, living in Antarctica. Who came up with the term "breezeway" anyways? "Freezeway" is definitely a more appropriate term. You know the ice has to be at least an inch thick on every inch of your old car and since your defrost barely works…you know you're in for a good ole' kick in the butt…but you're used to it right? Still though, wouldn't it be nice if you could afford one of those automatic car starters? Better yet wouldn't it be nice if you had a garage to walk out into in the morning? Even better yet…if you just had the money to stay in bed today…everything would be awesome. As you're thinking of the different unlikely scenarios which could make these brutal winter mornings better, you realize you forgot one possible major solution to this frustrating struggle…(not to worry though, you're about to be harshly reminded).

As you begin the tedious scraping process with your dollar store scraper, you truly wonder if you're making any progress…at all. You're not wearing gloves, because sadly, you know your fingernails are going to need to aid in the process. Unfortunately they have more power than your scraper…and your hands are as red as tomatoes every winter anyways, so no big deal. As you're manually scraping away, and believing you're on the verge of frostbite, your sweet, bundled up neighbor comes waltzing down the stairs. Oh yes, the lady that has the same exact car as you. No reason to be envious of her, right? Right…you're not being tested just yet this morning. It's not like she drives a Corvette….she drives a car JUST like YOURS, so not only are you not feeling boastful about having a better vehicle than her, you're DEFINITELY NOT feeling envious.

"See God?… I'm doing good, right?"

You wish it were that simple this morning…you really do…but sadly, you may be about to fail the envy test.

She stops, looks at you, and while flaunting her perfectly curled hair and gorgeously applied makeup, comments, "Oh wow, you have to scrape all that off yourself? It's soooooo cold out here this morning. I'm so thankful that my husband comes out and gets my car started, scraped off, and warm every morning…so that it will be ready for me when I need to leave."

You do that fake giggle that you're so good at, and say, "Oh I know it, and it's really funny…cause we have the same car and all."

"Have a nice day," she innocently encourages, and then speeds away in her perfectly warm, perfectly defrosted car, which suddenly looks so much more desirable than yours.

"Dear Lord…why can't I be her for just a few minutes?" you find yourself silently asking.

The fact is…she has a husband that protects her from the vicious wind chill that is currently colder than your last ex-boyfriend's heart. You want what she has!

Oh well, at least your car should feel a little better than the outside… you think to yourself once you've worked on it a good torturous five minutes. You did your best, and although you have tunnel vision while driving, you are ready to go. No, it's not like you have safe visibility or anything, but this will have to do. As you jump into your car, you wonder why it doesn't feel any warmer than outside.

Ohhhh…your heater is broken. Fabulous!

Before bursting out into your crazy laugh at the ridiculousness of the situation, and realizing you are 110% envious of your pampered neighbor, you pray:

"Dear Lord, can you please help me through this envy thing, get me to work safely, and keep my fingers from falling off because I'm not sure I've ever been this cold in my life…ever? Amen."

Harsh Leah Reality #36: Phone Blunders

(Reflection time yet again): Remember when you became so tech savvy or "text savvy" that you got cocky about it? Of course you do. Like most times when you get a larger than life ego about any given thing…

it comes back to bite you. Every time your friends pointed out that you were the world's fastest texter, you felt so cool in a nerdy sort of way. You respond in record time, and you normally avoid those potentially life scarring auto corrects.

You were also amazing at forwarding your short-lived ex-boyfriend Britton's texts to your friend Brittany. You'd put in some commentary along the lines of "What a stupid idiot!"

Or "I don't know why I want him back," or something like that.

You really shouldn't have been so confident that you weren't ever going to make a potentially brutal mistake. You can recall almost accidently forwarding his own message back to him instead of sending to your friend. Scarily, you even almost came close to texting him to complain about him once. However, you were always proud that you caught yourself before the damage was done.

Here you are annoyed, and needing to vent, once again. Hey, what's new? You notice a mushy gushy conversation that Britton and his new gal are having on his Facebook page, and you just cannot help but forward it to Brittany.

"Aww…look at this crap! They're just sooooo in love. I know I dumped him, but this REALLY bothers me.. Sometimes I'm afraid I want him back! I mean look what he moved on to…Kaylie is really pretty. Seeing that someone like her wants him, it makes me wonder what was wrong with me. I know I wasn't sure that I was the most attracted to him…we both know his disgusting teeth bothered me, but he had a really great personality…and for some reason I'm becoming more physically attracted to him suddenly," you complain.

You are expecting to get a sympathetic text back from Brittany assuring you that Kaylie is NOT prettier than you, that his teeth are a deal breaker, that you will overcome him, and that you're just going through a phase, and you can do so much better.

You do get a text back from a name that begins with Bri…but it isn't Brittany. It's Britton…the very person you were talking a mixture of affection and trash about.

"Wow, I don't even hardly know what to say...except you are shallow, I always hated that dark nail polish you wore, and we are NEVER getting back together...EVER," texts Britton.

At this rate, you know you are screwed. Completely and helplessly screwed...and you completely deserve it. The only humor in the matter is, you think of Taylor Swift with his "never getting back together ever" comment. Did he ACTUALLY mean to use that current famous line in his reply, or was it just all coincidental? Probably coincidental because there is no other way for him to explain his disgust towards you right now, except by saying that he is done with you forever.

You would reply if you had ANYTHING halfway good to say, but for the first time in your life...you have no good explanation, no witty comeback, and zero chance of recovery. You are currently the scum of the earth...and you deserve it.

Not surprisingly, Britton unfriends you from Facebook following the blunder, but he doesn't unfriend Brittany. A week later, Brittany informs you that his status says he is at the dentist getting a teeth whitening job done. Oh well, on the bright side...at least you helped the poor guy out. You only wanted him again because he wasn't available. Kaylie should thank you for this. You didn't accidently say anything about his slightly Groucho Marx-like eyebrows in the text though...so he most likely won't be doing anything about those. Maybe Kaylie will get the courage in a couple months to offer to help him pluck, when she is done shaping her perfect model-like ones. One can only hope anyways...

Harsh Leah Reality #37: The Everywhere Girl

You've always been pretty easy going, and for the most part, well-liked. Yes, you've dealt with the drama queens and the "I hope you fail" haters plenty of times...but it's just part of life no matter who you are. Often times, the worst part of being a woman is dealing with other women...plain & simple. We ALL know that for ANY woman who has EVER dated in her life, there is probably a woman out there who isn't so fond of her, and doesn't exactly wish her well...because the guy she is dating just happens to be this bitter woman's ex. It usually doesn't even matter if the bitter woman still wants the guy, or if she's long done with him...she will almost always still want to compete with the new woman.

You know the story: She stalks your Facebook – she says you have big hips, that your front tooth is crooked, that your eyes are too far apart, and that you're not THAT pretty if you look really closely. She looks through your 8,000 photographs just to be sure that you don't have anything over her. She confirms that you don't, but then needs reassurance five minutes later, so she calls her best friend to join in on the bash fest.

As of recently, there is a particular catty female who has really ruffled your feathers. "Ranella" is about as real as a three-dollar bill...and she's everywhere you look. You definitely have a love/hate relationship with the mutual friend option on Facebook, because any time you even casually start seeing someone, they just happen to be friends with her. On one hand you want to know, but on the other hand, you're aggravated and thinking, "HER again!?" Is there a guy in this town or heck, outside of this town, that she HASN'T tried to dig her claws into!? You've heard about the six degrees of separation, but you are starting to believe six may be too far apart. You thought you moved to a big city, but some days you feel like you never left your small town.

She could've chosen to move in on almost any man in town, but she chose yours. You're not sure if it's the six inch false eyelashes, her tan that looks like it came from a Dorito's bag, the hooker heels (not the cute stylish stiletto type), her unmovable hair, that Botox-abused looking mouth, or the high-pitched squeaky voice that won him over in admiration, but she accomplished her evil little mission. You're too good for this nonsense...you really are. You're also having a hard time with your "sweet" thought life once again.

You envision Ranella attempting to get her hands dirty, or spending just one day on the farm or at the factory like you've had to over the years. Just the thought makes you laugh out loud. You don't think the "ball cap, scoop up crap" kind of life is for her...nor is breaking any kind of a sweat, but it's sure entertaining to think about. Well, okay...maybe you're stretching it just a little. Tanning beds can get pretty hot, and since she roasts in one 24/7, she has therefore sweated in her life many times...or, maybe not. Maybe she really *is* buying a bottle of instant tan called "Dorito Diva." You can just imagine the "three easy payments infomercial" now. You're pretty sure her hair is a safety hazard and that hooker heels wouldn't make the dress code grade at the factory or on the farm. However, it would be pretty entertaining to watch her sink into some cow manure though, wouldn't it? On second thought, maybe not...because with as annoyingly high-pitched as her talking voice is, you can only imagine what her scream must sound like.

Ranella isn't the only "everywhere girl" that you've met in your lifetime though. No – it's definitely memory lane time here now, because there is a much longer-running "everywhere girl" in your life, and she's been there since junior high. You moved 250 miles away from her after high school, but it doesn't seem to be far enough. You are thinking that maybe America isn't big enough for both of you. Heck, sometimes you worry that planet earth isn't even big enough. She is a bitter woman to say the least, and she's never gone. You really should have been done with this "Anita" chick YEARS ago.

She was the girl who thought she one-upped you, because she dated your Jr. High boyfriend Matt right after you. She tried to get with him the ENTIRE time that you were with him. She wore water bras to school, severely broke the dress code (yet never got in trouble for it of course), and sported high heels that she looked like a newborn calf in, as she struggled to walk down the hallways. She flaunted herself at him right in front of you, as if she was trying to make YOU feel like you had no right to be with your own boyfriend.

It was clear that she had a special enticement for taken men... especially your man. She was undeniably waiting in the wings for the demise of your near perfect relationship. Much to her devilish delight, the breakup officially took place. Like a perfectly, intricately, iced double layer wedding cake slipping out of the baker's hands and crashing to the ground, she watched the collapse of a beautiful design with a sick smile on her face.

Two days after your first heart-wrenching, earth-shattering breakup which initially was mutual...you realized you weren't so ready to let go of your first love. The problem though? Anita, the most promiscuous girl five counties wide was officially ready to go in for the kill. The bigger problem? The apple of your eye was falling under her spell.

Once again, you've always been a sweet easygoing person, but just the sight of her sickened you, and you became increasingly nauseous every time that you were forced to witness their stomach-turning PDA. You really wanted to get back at her for what she was doing to you. Little did you know...you were about to get that chance.

Also, what you didn't know was that you and Anita had the sickness issues in common. Apparently your ex brought you up in nearly every one of their conversations, much to her dismay...but you wouldn't find this out until much later.

Long before the truth of him still being hung up on you came to surface, she developed an evil little plan on her own.

She signed on to his AOL Instant Messenger screen name. Yes, back in your junior high days, people got on AIM. "Stalkerbook" hadn't been invented just yet. Back then, AIM was the coolest thing since sliced bread. Anyways, one of your friends gave you a heads up that Anita was on his screen name, and warned that she may just end up messaging you.

Message you she did...and you were so prepared for her to do so. In fact, you were so excited that she did. You were immediately experiencing an adrenaline rush and more excited than a rat in Greenbay. As you heard the ding of her messaging you posing as "Matt," your recent bloodhound face evolved into a mischievous grinning face, which belonged to Valleywood school's new mean girl.

Immediately Anita began pretending that she was "your ex," wanting you back.

"I've been thinking about you baby. I miss you so much, and I think about you all the time. Will you please go back to me?" said Anita pretending to be your old flame.

Knowing you now had the ability to turn her world upside down… should you do it? Should you give in to the mean idea crossing your mind? OF COURSE YOU SHOULD! Though at the time you had zero idea that Matt actually missed you, you decided to take it upon yourself to report that he did. In fact, you wanted to report that he missed you so much that he couldn't even leave you alone. You wanted to paint the picture that your e-mails were overflowing with his regrets, that your mailbox couldn't hold anymore of his pleading letters, and that your family's landline was ringing off the hook from his persistent calls. None of that existed, but you knew you could force Anita to believe that it did. You knew Anita was looking to lure you in…to play a cruel joke, only to turn around and tell you it was all a prank…or perhaps, she needed reassurance that Matt wasn't still hung up on you. Either way… you were about to turn the tables, and you were about to be the captain of their now sinking relation-ship (no pun intended).

"Matt, I am getting really tired of you saying these things to me all the time! How many times do I have to tell you, you are with Anita! She would be really upset if she knew she's not your first choice. Please get over me, and please stop saying you want to dump her, and get back with me. I am done with you, and I'm not telling you again," you replied with a proud smile on your face.

Not surprisingly, hateful Anita had nothing to say back. She almost immediately signed off the chat. You can remember that beautiful sound of her signing off. You really just wanted to be a fly on the wall. You really wanted to see the disaster…but you couldn't. All you could do was sit back and wait.

Just as you were hoping, their "relation-ship" sunk and was never seen again…not a shred of survival was found.

However, unlike the ship, Anita would keep popping up…for years and years to come.

First things first though: Two months after Anita got a taste of her own medicine…you and Matt gave it another go, but this time, you wound up breaking HIS heart.

Now let's fast forward all the way to recent events. You are far from where you grew up, but you are currently seeing Scott from back home…from a different school than you and Miss Anita's old alma mater. Since you're currently in the beginning butterflies' stage of your new relationship, you make your weekend visit known on his Facebook. As you and Scott are spending a relaxing evening together, his phone dings as soon as he gets up to go grab something in the kitchen. You look down and see a familiar name come up on his screen: A name that you haven't seen in a good fifteen years. A name that takes you from sweetheart to raging psycho in 2.5 seconds.

Without hesitation, you say, "SCOTT! HOW do you know Anita Butte!?"

"She used to occasionally come to our high school basketball games when she was hooking up with one of my team members, but I never really knew her that well," he innocently replies.

What transpired the next 30 minutes was probably the worst tongue lashing that poor Scott has ever endured to this day…and we're not talking about kissing here. After you explained and re-explained the beyond aggravating history with this boyfriend burglar over and over and over in as many different ways as you could, you were hoping you got your point across.

"Well, she just started texting me recently," he insists.

"Ohhhhh…you don't say! No offense Scott, but she's interested in you because of me!?…okay!? You got that!? She still isn't over Jr. High. She's still obsessed with one-upping me! But I'll tell you what!? She needs to put on her big girl panties and get over it. This is an A & B relationship, so she needs to C her way out!? You got that!?" you warn.

"But, she needed my help with some electricity issues in the house, and I told her I'd do it," he confesses.

"Oh, cause there's NO electricians in the Eastern Kentucky area ANYWHERE, are there!?" you say enraged.

"Well, I tell ya what…I'll just tell her I can't now, and that she's going to have to get someone else," he offers.

"GOOD!" you say.

Miss Anita failed and it made you so very happy. However, you and Scott's breakup two months later didn't make you so happy. You ended it because like you often do, you lost interest in him. Either Anita is still waiting under the hoop for the rebound, or she's waiting to see who your next guy is. Just for the record – you are officially done with boys back home…forever.

Some women are just like boomerangs. They just keep coming back, no matter how far gone you think they are. It's "Mean Girls" times ten… you're just not sure which character bests fits you.

Harsh Leah Reality #38: Grocery Store Gawkers and Parking Lot Creepers

All this thinking about the past, present and future calls for some comfort food. You know how it goes. You're out of chocolate and donuts, and you need to head to the store to replenish your supply ASAP. Replenishing your supply means subjecting yourself to "Creeperville" at 10 p.m. Yeah yeah…so you cut things off with yet another great guy earlier this week, and you're having some doubts about your decision. Doubts call for some serious sweets and treats. As usual, your friends have been lecturing you over your latest poor decision of letting yet another good catch go. He was just getting too close to you too fast, and your walls went up. Despite your guilt over his sad social media posts and his pleas to give him another chance, you know you're never going to "feel it." Still though, the whole situation has made you so angry at yourself that you decide to sabotage your diet.

Don't you just love the grocery store gawkers and parking lot creepers who you must face on your outings? You just need a few artery clogging groceries at the store…that's all. Why oh why do these vultures think you're there for a date or an on the whim marriage proposal? Didn't you uglify yourself enough? You really thought these winners would find the no makeup, messy bun, and sweatshirt look "unattractive." You were wrong. Of course with you, a grocery store trip is never *just* a grocery store trip. You know how to find the gawkers and you know how to find the creepers.

As you walk in, you feel like you're a strange species. Those dang neon flashing arrows have returned once again, and they're following you throughout the store. Is there ANYONE normal in here tonight? The sick smiles and the prolonged stare-downs are more than you can take. Is the circus in town? Where oh where is my chocolate aisle? Suddenly you seem to have forgotten where *everything* is located in the store that you shop at more than once a week. With every step you take, you feel the glare, you feel the stare, and you just want to be home safe and sound…with your sweets.

As you're grabbing for your favorite candy bars, a decent looking 20-something-year-old guy gets extremely close to you as if he's looking at the same thing. He tells you that you smell good. Oh dear…just what you need: Grocery store love. At least there's a normal man in here though…maybe. He tells you that you're beautiful and asks for your number, and though you're hesitant to give it to him, you think "why not?" You aren't about to let him think you're truly back on the prowl though. So you say "thank you," and proceed to hunt for donuts.

Alas! You've found the donut display…and ummm, they're out of your chocolate sprinkle ones. You are completely outraged! You really should file a complaint with management over this nonsense! You are tempted to throw a toddler-like temper tantrum, but decide you probably shouldn't draw any more attention to yourself in this place. You guess the glazed ones will have to do. A donut is a donut. Sorta… but sprinkles are your favorite.

As you're getting ready to leave, the ultimate creeper whistles loudly, and tells you that you're as fine as wine. Ohhhh please. Is that all he's got? That one is reallyyyyyy going to win you over (sarcasm intended).

The second you get into the car, you hit the locks, and do a quick check in your back seat. Phew…you're fine, girl!

Two minutes later: Mr. Smell Good won't stop calling your phone.
Two hours later: Mr. Smell Good won't stop calling your phone.
Two days later: Mr. Smell Good won't stop calling your phone.
Two weeks later: Mr. Smell Good won't stop calling your phone.
Two months…Yeah, you get the picture.

Were the donuts worth this ongoing stalker? Well, at the time they were. Now, you're not so sure. Okay, donuts are always worth it. Always. However, you won't be giving out your number to ANYONE on your next run.

Harsh Leah Reality #39: Drive it like you stole it – The Backstory of Cheater Joe Limburtony (as promised)

In your phase of ongoing fierce independence, you find you are sometimes simply scarred by memories of your past. The more you reflect, the more you realize. The only one who ever brought you anything other than full-fledged pain was the boy next door. All the hurt Blake caused you stands out in your mind and the way Joe Limburtony disrespected you has left a deep wound. In an attempt to move forward, you share the full-fledged story of Joe Limburtony with your new friend Amber. Instead of crying, you and Amber wind up laughing hysterically and she high fives you for being so hard-core. Here goes:

Ever since you can remember, you have had the title of "good girl." Though you are far from perfect, you are for the most part decently behaved…so that's fine with you. However, people often mistake your moral convictions as meaning you're naïve or sheltered. What they don't know is good girls often have a knack for landing in bad situations… like possibly worse than the average "bad." For one thing, good girls love bad boys and bad boys love good girls. You know you shouldn't love these notorious characters, but they're a weakness. You laugh to yourself knowing you've landed in dangerous situations far more than the person declaring your extreme innocence, because you have at times surrounded yourself with the wildest of company in the worst of places, and taken the most hazardous of risks. They are completely clueless about your out of this world capacity for survival, or how many times you've dodged the bullet.

They don't know that back in the day, because of your ex-boyfriend you almost ended up behind bars in some not so fashionable black and white stripes (not the fun zebra print stuff, okay)? Hey, it was his fault that y'all were clocked as going 120 mph on his crotch rocket...not yours. Once you finally realized you were tired of his daredevil ways, you said your good-byes. You couldn't deal with the abnormal risks that went along with him anymore...though you felt kind of cool in your innocently reckless lawlessness.

You were once even pretty certain that his raging psycho ex-girlfriend was going to try to murder you, but other than that, you had no fear of danger. In addition to spending time with guys that had no regard for their reputation, safety, or their life, let alone yours, you were a professional player dater. You always knew you were dating players, but you liked lying to yourself. You chose to believe in the potential of what they could be, not what they were. Your detailed mind always laid all the cheating evidence out like a PowerPoint presentation, yet you didn't want to confirm the obvious. However, you've always been one to kick em' to the curb as soon as the obvious is proven.

Nonetheless, you think you missed your calling...as a detective. You don't like to brag or anything, but you're pretty dang smart at solving mysteries. You treat every man like the board game "Clue," and every site as a "crime scene." You're not good at everything in life though... you are horrible at Algebra, or really anything that mixes numbers and letters together. Well, you do a great job of adding up evidence to equal conviction. Seriously though, "people reading" is a skill of yours, but evidently so is overthinking. You try to not accept anything as truth until you have the evidence proving it to be. Anytime a friend's guy shows suspicions of cheating, you are always on it. This time, your strong suspicions were in your own relationship once again...and you weren't about to invest anymore time in someone who might not be taking you seriously.

You'll never forget when you were first lured in by Joe Limburtony (Yes, the one that later went on to be with your so-called friend Cami). Though your guard was up and almost no one could truly hold your interest at the time, you were allowing yourself to see where it goes. Everything seemed almost too good to be true, and maybe that is why your gut just wouldn't leave you alone. You kept sensing that something was just off. Six months into your relationship with him, you finally made yourself come to grips with the fact that he was almost certainly cheating on you. You found an earring in his car that didn't belong to you, came across a pair of women's shoes in his second closet (and you knew he wasn't into "THAT" sorta thing, and hey, they were way too small for him), but everything was adding up, and pointing to unfaithfulness. You didn't trust him since day one, but you just didn't want to give in to your gut. You also didn't want him to know that you were on to him. All of the signs were there and you knew it, but it didn't mean that you wanted to accept it.

You finally decide that you are sick of weighing out the "yes," "no's," and "maybe so's." You simply can't just dump the guy, because you really, really like him. He has that magnetic personality that always keeps you wanting more, and he has such a cute smile (though the Boy Next Door still has him beat in that category). Seriously though, if you could confirm you aren't sharing Joe with the entire community and you would never have to, you would definitely keep him…despite the fact that the red flags, blinking lights, and caution signs are everywhere.

After deciding that Facebook stalking will no longer suffice, you decide to check into what he's *really* doing on his night off. He claims he needs to do some Friday night house cleaning, but you just don't buy it. You know his house only gets cleaned because of you. You can't imagine him throwing away his chicken wing bones, or cleaning up his kitchen without you. You are pretty certain that you are being lied to. You've had some reasons for suspicions, and you know all too well from past experiences that intuition generally doesn't lie.

You convince a trusted friend to borrow her car, and to camp out with you for an hour in front of his alleged mistresses' house (No, this wasn't Cami). There's an abandoned barn across the road, which you investigate beside. The spying is going good for a while…or bad, because you see exactly what you don't want to see. His car did pull up, and his mistress ran out her front door and greeted him in an extremely non-platonic manner. At least you knew though.

You decide to stay just a little longer to collect necessary evidence, as if you don't already have enough. You have a reasonable view, and you're able to see them in her living room. You feel as inconspicuous as Casper in doing so, but you're not exactly feeling like a "friendly ghost." As you're camped out with binoculars and proud of yourself for being so recluse, you realize that you've been spotted by her neighbor, who may in fact be trying to protect Joe's cheating ways.

Your friend then screams, "Oh my gosh that guy is coming after us!"

Yep. You probably shouldn't have ignored that "no trespassing" sign.

You then realize THAT guy is one of Joe's friends who you know quite well. You then feel betrayed on more levels than one. You think he probably wants to find out if that is you in the car. He's right, but you aren't about to let him find out for certain.

You aren't sorry for trespassing and you aren't sorry that you went out to learn the truth. You're not about to let the wool be pulled over your eyes…nor are you going to let yourself get caught by the raging psycho coming at you full speed from across the road. Tires are spinning and stones are flying. You know you can either cower like a wimp, show your face, and admit why you're there, or you can take off like a crazy wronged woman on a Frappuccino- filled adrenaline rush…you choose the latter. As you are stumbling with your ignition, you tell yourself this is one of those times for extreme rule-breaking. This is a time to think faster than the speed of light.

The crazy watchdog tries his best to block you in, after flying towards you at full speed. With a rapid turn of the wheel to the right, you narrowly escape the barn and a head-on hit within inches. He swings open the door and jumps out to attack you, and or to scare the living daylights out of you, but you take this as an opportunity to outdo his sorry butt. Her vehicle isn't exactly supposed to be known for its power steering…but man, at this moment, you have it. Her little car is surprising both of you.

Without a second to think, you outsmart that sucker, and quickly take a different direction which watchdog isn't expecting. Your friend is praising your out of this world driving skills with her head still ducked down. You panic and remind her that you aren't out of the clear just yet. You then realize a second vehicle is after you, and that Joe is the driver. However, you FLY out of that lot, and "Lil' Red" decides to transport you through this high-speed chase with all of her might. Let's just say… after a half mile, you leave those suckers in the dust.

You are officially Wonder Woman behind the wheel, slicker than a NASCAR driver, and cooler than Grand Theft Auto. You drive that thing like you stole it. Your friend is now officially your real partner-in-crime.

You arrive home in one piece, and as you lie in the safety of your bed, you realize that Dorothy had it right, "There's no place like home."

You grin behind your coffee cup as you sneak into work the next morning unscathed.

Joe never did say anything to you about your camp out (though you're guessing it was on his mind when you saw him at the Valentine's Day outing with your ex-friend), and you never did say anything to him, but you did now have enough evidence to convict him as guilty… so you used the "this just isn't working out" line. To this day, he and his little watchdogs are probably still talking about the little blonde that got away…(pun intended).

You had indicators that Joe might be a player, but what you didn't realize was he has a better playbook than a pro athlete. Heck, he's the coach! Some guys just seem to share the Lay's potato chip slogan, when it comes to women: "You can't have just one."

Harsh Leah Reality 40: 33, Single & Free

Now it's time for another birthday. You tell the girls you don't really feel like going out this year. You think you're just going to stay in and reflect this time. Of course they find your desire for deep thought time to be the funniest thing they've ever heard. They remind you that you're 33, not 83. However, in your mind, you have entered a panic mode that far exceeds your late 20's crisis. Never mind that you've been reflecting for six months straight. You still need to spend excessive time in your head…you're convinced of it. To top it all off, you found a GRAY hair on that head this morning. No, your eyes weren't deceiving you. It was as gray…as your memory is suddenly becoming.

Despite your secret "freak-out fest" earlier, you let the girls bully you into a night out. You will be going to a nice dinner, and then to the movies for the latest chick flick smash. Deep down, you wanted to go from the get-go. Deep down, you wanted to be fed with unrealistic happy endings that would give you hope on your 33rd birthday. You're so glad you have friends to push you into things that you actually want to do, but would rather deny wanting to.

At dinner, you're presented with cards about getting old, comments about AARP, and 40 candles on your birthday cake. The whole 40 joke gets less and less funny every year, because it's getting closer and closer to being true. Once it's true, what will they move on to? 50? Oh well, you're still seven years away from the big 4-0. That is a good while away, right? Not really. Seven years flies, actually.

As you're sitting there watching the latest Hollywood phenomenon, you find yourself wanting to believe in love again. Then your mind becomes clouded with the past 17 years of your life. Your life has been the opposite of a chick flick, which has caused you to become somewhat apathetic to relationships…though you almost always *sorta* have someone. You never *really* have anyone it seems like. The older you get, the more set in your ways you become. If a guy just doesn't do it for you…he just doesn't do it for you. You're not settling for anything less than everything you want. Why? Because you know men like Channing Tatum, Ryan Gosling and Zac Efron exist.

As you're driving home for the night and contemplating softening your heart up to love just a little bit, you and your first boyfriend's old song comes on the radio. WOW…you haven't heard this one in years.

Suddenly, you're sixteen again, and you're thinking about marriage and babies again. Before you became this high-powered, fast-paced drifter, you were a quiet home-body who wanted nothing more than to have a husband and babies. Did you make a mistake by running from it, and running towards your dreams instead? Should you have broken his heart that day? Suddenly, you realize you've been in the dating field longer than you've been single. Maybe you just need a good ole' break?

Those memorable lyrics and that feel-good memory just won't leave you alone. By the conclusion of the song, you realize you made the right decision all those years ago. The music is timeless and your heart is also timeless in some ways. Father time says you're older, but somewhere deep within you remains that full-of-life teenager who believes in forever. Deep down, that girl has never really changed – but who she thought would be the one has changed. In that moment, you decide you will no longer date, let alone entertain the thought of anyone who isn't ready to give their all to you. Uh huh…that's right! You feel renewed, you feel free…

Sigh…the radar chip of *someone very, very special from your past* has just apparently went crazy, because *he* texts you. What starts with a happy birthday, concludes with, "Can I come over?"

Okay, so that whole thing about never settling for someone who isn't ready: *Maybe* he will change his mind and it soon won't be considered settling, or maybe you're already back to square one? Are you 33, single and free, or are you 33 and somewhere in between single and confused? The second one…definitely.

UNIVERSAL RELATIONSHIP STRUGGLES & MILLION DOLLAR QUESTIONS

I am officially back to being me - Holly Marie Tong, and you are back to being you.

Okay, so now we've visited 20 chick flicks lies, and we've walked through 40 of Leah Gardowski's brutally harsh realities. Now, it is time to meet somewhere in the middle, and to visit the authentic reality of today's biggest dating struggles, which often keep us from enjoying fairy tale-like endings. The disconnects, the misunderstandings, dishonesty, lack of communication, and the looseness of today's relationship realm, all seemed to combine as the causes of Leah's rough road. Maybe women like Leah and other good single folk (men included) could find what they're looking for if society as a whole would simply get it together? Maybe if people would always just say what they mean and mean what they say, the other person wouldn't spend hours, days, weeks, months, and years wondering what *really* went wrong or why things *really* aren't working. Maybe the dysfunctional relationship world would be somewhat functional if self-respect, respect for others, honesty, and communication were priorities of everyone in the dating pool? Let's take a look at some of the very issues which often push a person to wander in the wilderness as an unhappy single, or instead cause them to take the plunge with the wrong person at the wrong time. I'm not expecting to save the relationship world here, but humor me for bit..

Soooo…what should our relationship status say?

I don't know about you, but I believe the #1 struggle in today's dating world to be the dreaded "title" process of determining two people's relationship status. When I was 16, it went something like this: Boy meets girl. Boy tells girl he likes her and asks her out on a date. Date goes well. Boy asks girl to be his girlfriend. Girl agrees. They commit to an exclusive relationship.

I really thought that was all there was to it…I really did, but little did I know, time would show me a much more complex, red-taped, screening process. Yes, I'm now far from 16, but honestly, I miss the check "yes" or "no" letter days. It was so simple, so-straight up, and so very cut and dry. For me, today's dating world strikes the brain as more confusing than high school Algebra, and as foreign of a concept as French II class. Maybe this dates me, but I reminisce about the days of "going steady," wearing a guy's varsity jacket, and wearing his class ring around my neck, knowing that meant I was the only girl in his world. I am the sharing type when it comes to giving someone my last piece of gum, or giving up my sweatshirt for someone who needs it more than I. I also am always more than willing to share my time with a friend because they need someone to talk to, but when it comes to men…I definitely do NOT knowingly share. Notice, I said knowingly…*sigh*

Yes, the title earning ordeal feels like an intense, detailed certification and testing period which requires more hoop-jumping than a three-ring circus. Getting to know someone requires more studying than the bar exam, and in the end, it's a pass or fail. Like the good ole bar, today we are waiting several weeks, maybe a good three months to receive our determining result on what our next step is going to be. Lawyer or wanna-be lawyer? Exclusive or single? The waiting period for many, feels like a time of wondering if time is being wasted, or if a winning score is going to be achieved. While "seeing," "dating," "talking to," or "hanging out" with a guy, I find myself wondering if he is taking an imaginary red pen and keeping score by checking off anything I say which might not be the exact answers he's looking for. Admittedly, I'm using that red pen on him..

Since three months seems to be the common determination period (at least in Music City), one quarter of a year can easily be spent in an "undefined" relationship which may have zero direction or future. Sure we've got to date and feel a relationship out…some work out, some do not. However, whatever happened to deciding after a few dates if you're "all in" or "all out?" In high school, my understanding was that having a "girlfriend" or a "boyfriend" meant being invested and committed to giving a relationship an honest chance. It never had to mean rushing to the altar, nor did it even necessarily mean you'd ever make it to the altar, but it meant that you were committed. Apparently for many today though, a "taken" status requires a brutal "sign your life" away paperwork ordeal. It seems like every day, a new status is invented. Here are just a few paraphrased examples of the common confusing/troubling statements I hear women make these days:

"We're seeing each other, but I think he might also be seeing a friend of a friend. Therefore, I have two dates with two different guys lined up next week."

"Well, we've been hanging out for about three months. We're exclusive I guess…but we're not Facebook official."

"This guy I've just started dating is so confusing. I think he is still talking to his ex and possibly dating multiple people."

"They're still hooking up, but they're not together anymore. They've basically switched over to friends with benefits."

Seriously, people? Who can honestly keep track or decode what all of these statuses even mean anymore? Should this topic really be so complex that a whole book could be written on it? Perhaps…but don't expect me to author it…….Then again, don't rule it out either…

Fascination with the chase

About a year ago, I started feeling a little nostalgic. Instead of choosing a standby chick flick, I found myself resorting back to the Looney Tunes cartoons that I grew up watching and loving. I bought the DVD set, and popped in one of the discs on a Saturday morning. Much to my surprise, I realized that these fun little exaggeration snippets are more realistic and true of today's dating world than any lovey-dovey film or TV show I could ever find myself watching. Take Wiley E. Coyote and Road Runner for example. No it's not a romantic story by any means, but it is the perfect example of the classic "chase."

For years and years, Wiley E. Coyote relentlessly chases Road Runner. However, the poor Coyote can never seem to catch that speedy bird that he so badly wants to devour. He appears to have nine lives, is constantly injured, and does crazy stunts all in the name of "food." What our favorite Coyote character probably doesn't realize is…he's in love with the chase. It's not Road Runner that entices him nearly as much as the chase itself does.

To a viewer, it's a wonder how much patience and capacity for survival that the poor soul has. He jumps off cliffs, gets set on fire, experiences injuries that no one in real life would survive, spends his entire bank account purchasing Acme equipment (for way less money, he could go to the store and buy actual food), yet he never gives up. He is always in mad pursuit, and he is obsessed to say the least. Just like in real life, he shows that perfectly executed plans fail. The faster Road Runner runs, the more Coyote chases him, and the more he resorts to crazy measures to reach this hard-to-get bird.

The truth of the matter is, if Coyote ever actually "caught" Road Runner, the excitement and the entertainment of this popular cartoon would be over. I have an image of Coyote following his great victory: Of course, he would begin by enjoying his feast of Road Runner. However, I'm led to believe that he would probably stop half way through the feast, and wonder what he is going to do with himself next. Let's be real here: He has ruined his credit score over this stupid bird, because he spent about $20,000 on equipment, and $20 of meat is all he got in the end. I mean look at how skinny that bird is anyways…there's nothing to it! It probably wouldn't be nearly as fun anymore, and Road Runner probably tastes average. He could have gotten other birds easier (meatier ones), but he wanted a challenge, and now that he's won the game, he's bored, and wants the next great chase.

Same goes for Sylvester and Tweety Bird. The poor cat has a goose-egg on his head every two seconds, his fur gets burnt all the way off, yet he survives, and he endures Granny's constant beatings. You would think he would have some serious head trauma by now, if not be dead for the 100th time. The truth of the matter is, Tweety is a small little bird that Sylvester could inhale before the reality of catching him would even sink in. Humorously though, if you notice, every time Sylvester does catch Tweety, he never just shoves him in his mouth. He instead looks at him with those crazy eyes in disbelief that he's actually caught him. Then Tweety somehow always miraculously escapes, and the chase starts all over. Let's face it, Sylvester would be bored and have nothing to do with his life if he ever caught Tweety.

I didn't really take in all the lessons Looney Tunes was teaching us until I sat there as an adult watching it. Although far-fetched, these popular cartoons accurately demonstrate some real life principles, and I'm going to guess that they probably do so unknowingly. There never really was a happily ever after for Wiley E. Coyote or Sylvester in getting the one that they kept chasing.

As humans, we constantly chase that which hurts us, no matter what the cost. As children, we enjoy the chase as we watch our favorite animation characters try to catch one another. As adults, we grow up to seek challenges which result in suffering injuries, playing our hearts like they have nine lives, and getting ourselves hurt over and over again. It is the chase which entices us. We often see the object as prey, but once we get them, the excitement often soon wears off.

The Great Pressure of Time

We often fall into the time pressure. If you're anything like me, when you were a little girl you planned out your future once or twice. I remember saying something along the lines that I would meet the right man at 21, be engaged by the time I was 22, be married by the time I was 23, and have my first child at 25. I imagined the perfect house, the perfect car, and the perfect life. As we get older, we somehow still tend to believe that love follows a time guideline. However, if you're among my "unmarried" readers: Please don't allow time or age alone ever, I mean ever, to determine your path and your future. Life may be way too short to not enjoy love, but it's also way too long to wake up next to someone every morning that simply "will do." I have come to believe that I would rather be single my entire life, than be with someone I'm not sure about.

Maybe you're nearing 30 and you still haven't found your prince. Heck, maybe you've long surpassed 30. No matter what your age may be, do not settle for the first candidate who you pass on the street simply because "it's time." Do not decide that you have to meet your match at the university in which you are pursuing your degree. I for one attended a private, Christian university, in which it is a common joke that women attend these types of institutions for their "Mrs. Degree." I was one of the minority students that escaped the door without a left hand ring. I do not regret that. During and after my time there, I was able to witness the marriages of many happy couples who met there, and genuinely seem like they're made for one another. Therefore, I am not downing these types of situations as a great possibility. He may rightfully be there, but please do not decide that he *has* to be there. Do not decide that you absolutely *have* to walk out of there with a ring. If you don't find anyone to knock you off your feet, don't scrounge the choices in front of you until you find one that "will do."

You may be in Tennessee and Mr. Right may be in Washington State. Maybe you're meant to meet him later on in life. Please do not think for a second that Mr. Right most certainly has to be in your small town of 300 people. He may very well be, but again, please do not decide that you *must* meet your match there. This doesn't mean you should automatically hop onto an online dating site and began searching other states. Studies have shown that a vast majority of the population does end up marrying someone who they've known for years, but that isn't the case for everyone. With that said, keep your possibilities open, and be aware of your endless surroundings. Ladies, it's a big world and thus there are more men out there than we can ever imagine. Guys, it's a big world and thus there are more ladies out there than you can ever imagine.

God is the "knowing one" writing your story, and carefully planning your future. God created all of us differently, which means our timing and our paths must also differ. We all have different personalities, dispositions, characteristics, wants and needs. Some may know who and what they want at a fairly early age. Young love is a sweet admirable situation, but if this hasn't been you, you are certainly not alone - so please do me a favor and do not fret over it. Some are meant to have their free rein for a while, so that they may discover, grow, and find out who they really are.

As for me, I passed my original "time frame" quite a while ago. Does this ever bother me and cause me to ask myself the all too common questions of:

Is it too late for me?

Will I spend my entire life alone?

Of course it has and sometimes still does, but ultimately I know I am waiting for something I haven't yet found, or perhaps, maybe I have found him, and the timing has been off. I could have chosen to settle down more than once with a guy who I could possibly "live with," but I am instead waiting for the one I cannot live without.

The problem of choosing someone that we can simply "live with" in most cases is that eventually this premature settling will turn a once tolerable situation into a very unhappy one. Sure most women are worried about security, having someone to share life with, someone to care for and protect them, but please do not let this "want" cause you to take a step that you are not ready for. If you are staying in a relationship or contemplating going into a marriage simply because you think it is time and you are trapped in some sort of an hourglass, do not, I repeat do not make this mistake. I personally choose to be as content as possible with where I'm at. Does this mean I'm never lonely or that I'm always completely content with my circumstances? Of course it doesn't, but I stand by the fact that time and age alone should never determine our relationship decisions. I wholeheartedly believe in individual timing and defining moments.

Peer Pressure...Not just for Young'uns Anymore

Oh yes, good ole' peer pressure. It is that very elementary, yet very universal term which we all learn at an early age. Let me tell you though, peer pressure is not just for young'uns anymore. Don't believe me? Perhaps, you have a large group of friends and you are the only single one in your group. Likely, your friends probably lovingly tease or always want to help their poor single friend achieve the same happiness as they have. As a result, they are always trying to set you up on blind dates, whether that be with their brother, cousin, or the new guy at their work. Have you ever experienced "third wheel syndrome?" I have. What about not having a partner for the board game in which your friends are playing? I have. Have you ever experienced an awkward Valentine's Day in which someone pressured you into spending it with someone you were not sure you wanted to date? Again, I have.

My favorite type of peer pressure though, or should I say my least favorite type of peer pressure, is the famous "you really need to meet my brother, son, or grandson" line that comes from outside your close group of friends. It's especially great when you've only known the person whom is hoping to change your relationship status for a whole five minutes. While it's flattering that someone would so quickly approve of you to meet their loved one and be a possible love interest, it's an utterly agonizing moment in many instances.

Did I enter the room with a shirt that said "single and miserable?" Again, I am not downing this as another great possibility, and these sweet people are usually just trying to be helpful. People meet in a wide variety of environments and situations, and this is a common one which has worked out beautifully throughout history. I know many people who have met their spouse through a family member, mutual friend, etc. If you're anything like me though (depending on who is offering to set me up), whenever I hear this famous line, I feel the anxiety building.

For one, how do they know that I would be attracted to their brother, son or grandson, and two, what are the chances that two people paired together by someone else will just instantly click?

Is it going to be a pressure filled situation when they introduce him to me?

Will he get hurt if the attraction isn't mutual?

Will I get hurt if the attraction isn't mutual?

Will everyone be mad at me if I do not want anything beyond meeting him the one time?

Will this make my new-found friendship or social relationship awkward with his mom, sister or grandmother?

Just the thought of the "he said, she said" telephone messenger game is enough to make me break out into hives.

With that said, don't get me wrong…when certain friends of mine want to set me up…I'm all for it, because I know they know what I'm looking for…but then there's those friends who *don't* know what I'm looking for.

Deal Breaker or Compromise Maker?

While it is true that you will never find perfect, and true that love is far from being all hearts and flowers, stand your ground and refuse to lower the bar. I'm not suggesting that you think of yourself as better than anyone else. Frankly, if any of us believes we are better than everyone we meet, maybe we need to pay more attention to our reflections in the mornings. I also am definitely not suggesting that you nit-pick every single detail about every single prospect. His nose is slightly crooked…true, but hey, maybe your bottom teeth aren't completely straight anymore either. When you love someone, you love their imperfections right along with them.

Perhaps, you were hoping to marry a lawyer and Mr. Prospect is a construction worker, or an undertaker instead of a delivery room doctor, or maybe he's an accountant rather than the musician you've always dreamed of? Is he worth making the simple adjustment of your original occupational hopes? If he's a good one, he definitely will be. Every great man is different from the next great man you meet. It's what makes the world go round. As long as he enjoys his occupation, he's good at it, and he brings home a pay check – isn't that all that matters?

Maybe you're athletic and Mr. Prospect isn't? Can he at least semi-dribble a basketball and toss the baseball from the mound to home plate, and do you at least connect well on other levels? Maybe he isn't an athlete, but you both enjoy church, good music, cooking together, and watching movies on Friday night.

Maybe you liked dark hair and his happens to be blonde. Is he still attractive to you? If so, maybe you can stand to ease up on your original plans for hair color. Maybe the fact that you're falling for a man with a different hair color than the usual proves he is extra significant. When thinking about this concept, I'm lead to remember country music singer Andy Grigg's hit song, "She's More." In this song, the man realizes that while many physical features and characteristics of this special woman are opposite of what he originally wanted, he knows "she's more" than he ever wanted. I've seen this happen many times!

Are you truly being too picky or does pickiness have no limits when it comes down to it? After all, when you marry someone you do owe it to yourself, and to them to be madly in love with them. If you're going to wake up next to someone every morning for the rest of your life, shouldn't you be as picky as you care to be?

So what should be a deal breaker and what should be a simple flaw that you simply can look past? I can't say that I have a direct answer for this, and honestly, I do not believe that anyone should claim to be an expert in this area, but here's my take: If you seriously cannot stand how he chews his food and it's going to bug you every day for the rest of your life -possibly pushing you to a divorce - maybe there are other underlining factors beneath the surface causing you to deem this annoyance as such a deal-breaker. If you absolutely cannot live with this flaw, maybe you're not cut out to marry and love this man for a lifetime?

For another example, there's that hat with the sweat stains and that worn out t-shirt he always wears, and you swear he does it just to get to you. A woman in love may gripe about his wardrobe, but most likely, she will not toss these favorites even if given the chance. I know, I know… some of you would and it doesn't mean you're not in love, but a woman in love often secretly loves the sweat stained hat though she claims to hate it. However, I am just generalizing. Anything you can learn to live with and maybe even learn to love is a compromise maker. Anything that is absolutely crippling your chances of a happy relationship which cannot be looked past is a deal breaker. Do not look for "perfect," instead look for "perfect for you!"

Independence…yet again

So, back to that independence thing we were discussing earlier. Did you notice how over time Leah became increasingly independent? As time tick-tocked on, and she continued to have one failed relationship after another, she became stronger each time, and eventually realized that she could take care of things on her own. It was also clear that she was even becoming somewhat set in her ways, and increasingly stubborn and proud in the process. She was trying to convince herself that she didn't even need a man's help anymore. After what she had been through, who could really blame her for her increasing self-sufficiency? Though men claim they love independence and a woman who can stand on her own two feet, it's also true they want to feel needed. They only want a woman's strength to go so far. Men typically want their lady to be strong enough to take care of her own obligations when needed, but soft enough to melt in their arms.

Sadly, Leah's "I don't need anyone" attitude in #33 is the very attitude which could be her enemy in future relationships if allowed to escalate. Though her strength and independence may initially attract a man, her over the top, hardcore ways are likely going to send him running for the hills sooner or later. Who's to blame for this? Both Leah and her sorry ex-boyfriends are to blame. Yes folks, in these types of situations, both sexes are generally to blame. Leah's problems generally started with her going for the very man whom she shouldn't have went for. She could never force herself to love the other guy who probably would have treated her better, thus she whines over the relationship which was destined for failure from the get-go. Predictably, the bad news guy proceeded to break her heart.

You've got to feel sorry for Leah though, because she can't necessarily help how her heart feels. She can of course help what she does about her emotions, but you can't force what you don't feel, and staying away from toxins is easier said than done. You've got to feel sorry for her next prospect because Leah is going to be one heck of a challenge. She now has trust issues, and thinks she can conquer the world without a man's help. If the last guy hadn't screwed her up, she likely wouldn't be "impossible" for this guy to take on. Leave a woman single long enough and she won't even know how to accept any sort of help or pampering. If she wasn't used to it before, it is going to feel like an unnatural foreign concept. In these kinds of cases, both parties are to blame, yet Leah's issues come with valid reasoning.

While it's very true that some women have proven to themselves and others that they are very capable of making it on their own, it is also true most of those women still prefer having a man around. Sure, us single women have become strong and successful, and we know how to take care of ourselves, but deep down a majority of us still want to make room for another person. It's in our human nature to love and to be loved. Leah obviously still had the desire for love in her heart all the way to harsh reality #40, but over time she accrued baggage which impeded her personal growth. Sometimes we've just got to share the weight. Every hardworking woman owes happiness to herself and to some lucky man whom she may have already met or have yet to meet. While some prefer the journey alone and are very comfortable with flying solo, most of us prefer to share life with another, despite the challenges we might face in putting ourselves back out into the lion's den.

It's very true that women are completely capable of opening up a door themselves, or even buying their own dinner, but it's also true that somewhere out there chivalry is still alive for our appreciation, despite its decline. It's a comfort to know that someone cares enough about you to do something sweet for you, not simply because you need it, but simply because they want to and because they respect and appreciate you.

While it's true some men may find extreme independence intimidating, it is also true that an independent woman can find a man who understands her "independent past." Yes single ladies. Somewhere out there…is a man willing to work with you. The needy, clingy type probably isn't your ideal soul mate. However, somewhere out there, is a strong man who has learned to live on his own, yet wants to share his world with someone else. This is the kind of man who will understand you, and accept you for who you are. Yes, it is absolutely possible to find your happy medium: You can keep your individuality, yet you will have to learn to share with another person.

In a nutshell, I believe there to be two main types of men when it comes to the "independent woman issue." Both types can be in a healthy, understanding relationship. There are those who seem to prefer a strong woman over a needy one. They are very attracted to not only confidence, but also to extreme assertiveness, and the go-getter nature in a woman. This is usually the type of man who has been independent himself. This scenario is common for those who marry post-college and oftentimes fall in the 30ish range. These are generally the types of couples who occasionally like their space. She may go on a weekend trip with the girls, while he may want a weekend to watch football by himself. If their interests are different, it's fine by them. They generally lead somewhat separate lives, yet they still manage to have a healthy, trusting relationship. They understand one another and their need for alone time. Therefore, it works out beautifully so long as they still spend a reasonable amount of time together.

The second type of man I believe there to be is probably the most common type: This is the man who appreciates a woman who can function on her own, yet likes her to strongly rely on him as well. He wants to do most activities with her if possible, and doesn't feel the need for much space. It is very important to him that they share common interests, and participate in those interests together, whereas guy #1 takes those differences as a chance for some healthy space. He may trust her fully, but this couple generally does most things together.

Both guys probably prefer to be the fix-it man and the one to take care of all of the "manly stuff."

Both relationships are different in their approach, yet with the right ingredients, both relationship styles are healthy. There's a third style out there in which the woman isn't allowed to have *any* independence or space, but this style is plain unhealthy.

The struggle between independence and dependence is a universal one, and there can be a fine line between the two. That fine line can often determine whether or not a relationship works. Independence is quite obviously one of the most common themes in the best-rated chick flicks. Take "The Wedding Planner" for example. There she is…the typical single, professional, successful woman wrapped up in her work. It's not that she goes unnoticed, as her ability to appeal to others is not the issue. The issue is she needs to find a man she loves, and of course, you can always rely on Hollywood to make that happen!

Do fairy tale-like loves exist?

It is all too common to think of giving the hope of a great love up, and then be overcome with the temptation to pop in "Sleepless in Seattle," or the opposite entitled, "While You Were Sleeping." Why is it on the very day we say we are done with relationships (or one of the many confusing statuses at least), we feel the need to watch a chick flick?

Who can truly deny they find hope in these movies?

Who can deny even through all the tears, complaining, and fretting over men, all they really want is their own fairy tale?

The question is what is a fairy tale?

Is a fairy tale something that we create, or is it something which has already been created for us?

Are we just not looking hard enough?

Wait, can real-life fairy tales even exist?

As a single lady, I obviously have not found a fairy tale per se. If I had, you wouldn't be reading this book right now. First of all though, let me set the record straight: Of course fairy tales do not exist if we're talking about enchantments, glass slipper fittings, fairy godmothers, and a beast turning into a man (well, that one is debatable I suppose). Seriously though, if "fairy tale" automatically means "perfect," and that everything is all hearts and flowers…forget it. If by fairy tale, you mean it is possible to find someone loyal who loves you just as much as you love them to where you can spend the rest of your life with them – then yes, I personally believe they exist. Now, before I sound like a gigantic contradiction, and you toss this "false advertisement of a pessimistic book" into the corner to collect dust, please let me explain my take just a little more.

In real life, "happily ever after," may feel more like "happily never after." Nonetheless, it can be your version of a fairy-tale. Yeah, yeah I know…you didn't exactly have to take "Dating 101" to grasp these concepts, but hey, sometimes we all need reminders when we've been drinking too much of that sugar-filled "Chick Flick Kool-Aid." That dang stuff is good though…trust me, I know.

As much as I have dreamed of fancy gowns and the horse and carriage, I have learned that in real life, red carpet events, designer stilettos, and an attractive wealthy man isn't the winning happiness formula. Sure it can't hurt if all the luxurious qualities are there, but if the most important qualities are not, then rest assured, the glitz and glamour will soon wear off. A mansion on the hill is cold, lonely, and drab if you don't feel loved in it. Dating a spotlighted heartthrob loses its shine if you know you're not his only heartthrob. Receiving real diamonds means nothing if the man presenting them to you is a fake. Yes, ladies it's true…a woman will be happier in a one room shack with a loyal, loving man than she will ever be with a cheater in a 7,000 square foot oceanfront property situation.

In a real life fairy tale, princesses are not exempt from stressful jobs, monthly cramps and poor bank accounts. Prince charming is probably going to leave those socks lay around, ESPN is likely going to occupy his Saturdays, hunting may not just be a hobby but rather a way of life, and he just may love wings even more than your home-cooking.

A real life fairy tale doesn't always start out as all butterflies and fireworks like we see in the movies. I for one, do not believe in "love" at first sight, and cannot be convinced to. I do, however, believe in "connection" at first sight. There are times when two people are instantly drawn to one another and something just "clicks." Actual love though, at least in my personal learning experience, comes from trying to understand one another, learning together, laughing together, and growing with one another. You cannot truly love until you have loved selflessly, until you have listened, learned and appreciated a person for far more than just their outer appearance. Their story and their sharing of their heart is what ultimately will determine true, lasting love. True love will always grow from getting to know one another through good times, bad times, trials and turning points.

Even the "connection at first sight" feeling can be unlike any feeling a person has ever felt before, and can tempt a person to automatically deem it as "love." I can personally think of three instances where I met a man, and we had that "moment" where I knew he was going to be part of my life in some way. He felt it and I felt it. In one instance especially, the connection was out of this world. It was as if the world stopped spinning for a minute and it was just him and I lost in the moment. Yes ladies, I did end up having a relationship with all three of these "connection at first sight" men at different points in my life, but none of them have made it to the altar. Meeting each of them was one of those unforgettable, significant happenings which caused my guarded heart to gush with excitement, but *at this point*, none of them are my forever. When an instant deep connection relationship comes to an end, it can be an extra hard pill to swallow, but God always has a way of healing that void, and bringing that new relationship which will trump the previous. Admittedly I'm still waiting on "that." Hey, timing can just be off sometimes too, right? Okay, moving right along…

Thought the first date went GREAT?

Anyone who has been a member of the dating world for more than one day is familiar with all the emotions which take place on a first date. However, one common emotion is the classic "buzz kill" one can receive after having an AWESOME first date with someone, feeling the butterflies, the connection and the chemistry…but not hearing from that person the next day, or the next three days…or perhaps… ever again. During the 72 hours of waiting on a call or text which never comes, the typical mind goes something like this:

Is he doing the "three-day rule?"

Did he change his mind?

Did I misread his signals?

Is he playing games?

Is he scared?

Did his ex pop back up?

Is he having second thoughts?

Oh my gosh…is he okay!?

There are a million possible reasons as to why he may not be calling, but it is probably for only one simple reason…a reason which you are probably not going to be able to easily decode. No matter what the reason, he still will get in touch with you sooner or later if he really wants to. The right man won't let you get away…at least not for too long.

The silent wait is a common anxiety both women and men all over the world go through every day and every hour following first dates. However, the stress doesn't end after date one, even if a phone call is received. Some people even complain that they often make it to a second date, but not to a third. It seems safe to say that modern dating can feel like a job interview. Getting asked to come in for round one (AKA date one) means you're being considered, and getting asked to come back for round two (AKA date two) means you're *really* being considered. Passing round two generally means you just may be earning yourself the exclusivity title, as long as he's the committing type. Until most people pass round three, they typically do a lot of thinking in between – a lot of rehashing and a lot of questioning. The post-date thinking process often goes something like this:

"Well…I think it went well."

"Well…I mean he seems to like me."

"He's hard to read. He said this which makes me think he wants a relationship with me, but he also said this which makes me think I could be friend-zoned."

Okay, that's enough of this agony for the moment. In the final section, we will be revisiting the "men who never call" issue.

Advice from ten different friends equals ten different thoughts

When one's love life is turned upside down, the normal, universal human response is to live it, breathe it, talk about it to all their friends, and maybe even to some other random people. Of course a girl often feels she needs to get advice from her girlfriends, but she also commonly believes she needs opinions from the male species as well, because they can hopefully decode this new difficult guy in her life. Has anyone else ever noticed though that advice from ten different people equals ten different thoughts? You know – when you're talking to the girls, there's one friend who will give it to you straight even if it breaks your heart, then there's Miss Sugar-Coater, Miss I Don't Know, Miss Indecisive, Miss Optimistic, Miss Pessimistic, and Miss All Men Suck, etc.

Any way you slice it, advice from ten different friends typically equals ten different thoughts and opinions. Relationship struggles can make a person desperate for answers, which may in turn cause them to look for answers or advice in places which they wouldn't normally do so. A hurting person sometimes has the habit of making a permanent decision on a temporary feeling, and in this case, they just may be telling too much to a not-so-trustworthy person. It may seem like a good idea at the time, but will it be in the long run? Will they be the reason for future relationship drama? Do they really actually care about your situation, or are they just being nosy about it?

In all honesty, girls…sometimes we have to stop and look at where we are seeking advice:

Do you go to one or two trusted friends, or are you sharing your problems with the community?

Do the people giving you the advice share your morals and values?

Are they gossipers who speak ill of other people, or are they known to be caring and trustworthy?

Remember Leah's dilemma at the bridal shower? EVERY friend told her something different regarding her breakup with Luke. Most of her friends probably meant well, but they were ALL actually wrong about their diagnosis. Of course her friend Cami who called her "too picky" and told her she was setting her standards too high, was later the very same friend that was apparently always after Leah's later former boyfriend Joe. Cami was supposed to be Leah's gal pal, but later on in their so-called friendship, Cami and Joe just happen to be seated behind her on a Valentine's Day date. Evidently, Cami wasn't always out for Leah's best interest. Her earlier advice to Leah about lowering her standards seemed like more of a discouragement than anything, which makes sense since it later came out that Cami wasn't a true friend.

Sometimes what we think will make us feel better simply doesn't. If the person you're seeking advice from constantly raves to you about how wonderful her husband is (when you in fact know differently), she probably isn't who you need to be talking to. Then there's the girl who brags that her boyfriend is about to propose right as you're pouring out your heart. Sure it's cool to share the good news, but could she wait a second and have a little compassion? Of course there's also the girl that has to compare EVERYTHING…absolutely EVERYTHING you say to her guy, when you know your guy is NOTHING like her guy. Yes, if you feel the need to share too much with the world, just be prepared to end up more confused, and more upset than what you were when you set out to seek advice.

Random internet advice is also another great way to drive a sane person insane. Reading the message boards and discussion columns can actually be quite entertaining. Just know that for any dating question you type into Google, you will find a million different opinions for each of your million questions. Okay, maybe thousands instead of millions in some cases…but seriously people, you're probably not going to find what you're looking for on there. Most of the advice/opinions I've read regarding "confusing relationships" seem a little off or just plain inconsiderate to me. The comment section is full of blatantly harsh replies without the responder even truly knowing much of what the poster is experiencing. The bold counselors, who have a vague story to go by, usually reply to the advice seeker in this kind of a way:

"Forget about him!"

"Move on!"

"He probably changed his mind."

"I don't think he likes you."

Though most answers differ, most of them have one thing in common: They are downright abrasive. Sadly, the "let it go" advice isn't so easy to hear for the newly heartbroken gal pouring her heart out. Also, her situation may be an unusual case. Though most male actions or lack of actions have universal meanings, they can't all be clumped into one category, or necessarily decoded by one know-it-all.

However, on the flip side, there are the classic internet advisors who mean well, but simply offer a tempting serving of false hope:

"My husband didn't call me till two weeks after our first date, and now we're married. So hang in there! I bet you anything that he's going to call."

"He probably lost his phone, girl."

"Guys like the girl to pursue. I know you say he's ignored your past three calls, but your persistence is going to pay off." (PLEASE do not listen to this one especially, girls).

In all honesty, I don't think anyone has ALL the answers, except God himself. My ultimate advice to you in this non "how-to" book is to say your prayers, take in his word, and keep your "sharing circle" small and wise.

Social Media TMI = The new depressant

Okay...so now, for another strong dose of truth. You know those times where you're slightly annoyed by something, but you cannot admit it, because if you did, everyone would think you're simply a jealous person? It's one of those sensitive subjects which a person must tread carefully with. However, sometimes it needs to be said...so here it goes:

There really does need to be a "Too Much Information" (TMI) button on Facebook. Alright, Little Miss Perfect Sheila, that just had another baby with her perfect hubby, I am happy for you sister. I perfectly understand that a frequent status update of yours is going to entail talk about your hubby and your children, and if I were married with children, I'm sure I would occasionally like to share my blessings as well. I love seeing happy families. It's refreshing and it gives me hope. However, there comes a point where you're just pouring on the sugar so thick that I'm sitting behind my computer gagging from overdose and seriously thinking about defriending you, girl. It's not the fact that you post twenty pictures of your new baby every day, or that you love your husband. You're proud of them…that's a loving mother and wife.

However, you're crossing the line just a little bit when I read updates like this in my newsfeed, every single time I login:

"My amazing hubby made me breakfast in bed, then washed all the dishes, then cleaned the entire house, and told me I was his "Cuddle Bear" forever and ever. Braden then pooped his diaper and it was the worst we've ever had…but once again, my amazing hubby stepped up to the plate. He got through changing the poopy diaper, and then Braden pooped all over the place again, and had to be re-changed again. It smelled so horrible it almost knocked me over. I told my hubby "you're so sexy when you're changing diapers"…to which he replied, 'I'm only sexy when I'm with you.' Then we kissed, and our three year old said, 'Eww!' Hehehehe…LOL."

So maybe I didn't copy a friend's status word for word, but yes, I have read postings just as sugary and syrupy as this one…Not to mention, gross! Yes, babies poop…but who really needs to hear every detail about your child's bowel movements? I realize there can be funny stories here and there regarding some memorable moments which may have a bit of the "yuck factor," but folks, statuses like the above one…c'mon now. Some things are just better left unsaid. Call me bitter, cynical, or call me whatever you like, but I KNOW I'm not the only person who gets annoyed by these over-the-top shares. I'm one of the few who are brave enough to admit it.

If you are near my age, slightly younger, or older, you know what I mean when I say we are at that time in our lives where a majority of people are getting married and having babies. Our newsfeeds are overflowing with a weekly update of a woman's pregnant belly, ultrasound pictures, and baby room pictures, which is totally cool, but aren't some of the "extreme" topics better left private? Well apparently not for everyone…

So yeah, maybe Facebook sometimes has the potential to be a little bit of a depressant for the single or the dysfunctional relationship crowd.

That's just the sugar-free truth. The everyday Facebook newsfeed goes something like this:

"Someone" went from "single" to "in a relationship" or "in a relationship" to "single." If you keep on scrolling, you will likely land on an encouraging photo quote. A good example would be the classic, "Someday someone will walk into your life and make you realize why it never worked out with anyone else." (Yep, anyone else hear that one a million times? Is anyone else starting to doubt it?) Of course though the first two items in the newsfeed are two separate pictures of the hands of two separate girls with engagement rings saying, "I'm engaged!," If you keep scrolling you'll run across a picture of someone's fiancé with a large paragraph stating how much they love him. Then someone else is posting a picture of their baby saying he's the cutest baby ever. Also, Jennie Jackson's dog is better than everyone else's dog. Someone else is feeling "old" by going into her old college bars (since I'm about the same age as her – that reminded me I'm old, too). Another friend wants to snuggle with her hubby and kids. Yeah, sometimes after seeing all those things in one sitting, a girl just has to click the log out button, because she's suddenly the outcast on Facebook.

Yes, Facebookers, it's the epidemic of every profile picture being a wedding photo, a photo of children, and every status being a "my hubby is so amazing status." It is also a "my kids are the smartest kids," and "I'm the most domesticated woman on the face of the planet," world we're living in. I'm not knocking it…if and when I get married - I expect I will probably post sweet little things here and there myself. It's natural and healthy to speak highly of your family and to be thankful for your blessings. It's good to be happy, it's good to broadcast it from time to time, and you frankly shouldn't have to really consider what anyone cares or thinks in the midst of your happiness. You are entitled the right to shout it from the rooftops.

However, it doesn't change the fact that somewhere there is a single person sitting behind a computer thinking, "wow, I am outnumbered." Whether my fellow singles want to admit it or not, at some point, most of us do compare ourselves to others who we think are ahead of us in life. It can become a focusing on the "have-nots" kind of moment. Plain and simple, Facebook can be the fastest way for a single to feel bad about oneself. If and when that happens, it's probably a good idea to disconnect for a bit. Nope, it's not the fault of the married mother who is blissful and deserves her happiness, but truthfully, reading a constant around the clock newsfeed update about family doesn't make it any easier for the single, kid-less woman to accept and embrace her status and place she's at in life. It also causes people to question the legitimacy of these relationships where one must constantly tell everyone how out-of-this world amazing their man is. If you're reading this, and you're one of my Facebook friends, and you think you're guilty as charged, you're probably not. I haven't defriended you, so that's a good sign. We're simply going over universal struggles for the non-taken folk here. You're all good, my dear social media kings and queens.

Okay, so just maybe whenever I see a newly married photo on Facebook, I can hear the song, "Another One Bites the Dust" playing in my head. Please don't hold that against me. I'm just continuing to be honest here.

Blue jeans and compatibility

It interestingly recently occurred to me that trying to find the right guy reminds me of shopping for the right pair of jeans. Some of the worst fitting jeans appear to be the most appealing on the clothing rack – they look great, stylish, and trendy – but when I haul them off to the fitting room, there is a serious disconnect. They don't feel right, and I'm simply not comfortable with them. I definitely wouldn't want this pair to be "that" trusty pair of jeans which I'm stuck with for years to come. Suddenly, they don't even look right, and I wonder how I was attracted to them in the first place. However, when I find that one right pair – I know it. They fit me just like a glove. We connect, I'm comfortable, and they will be with me a long time. We are compatible, and we "get" one another.

Yes, folks, I'm comparing jean fitting to relationship compatibility. I realize it seems a bit extreme, as buying a pair of jeans is much less serious than committing your life to someone, but it is a *fitting* analogy (pun intended). In case you're wondering, I DO have a favorite pair of jeans, and they've been with me for years upon years. I occasionally find a pair I like, but my "good ole' faithfuls" are hard to beat. They never let me down. Okay, you get the point. Some dates can appear to have all of the potential in the world, yet those two people just might not fit…at all.

My guideline is, I won't go on a second date with any man who doesn't compliment me as well as my favorite jeans. Many of the dates I have been on are like those awful super low-rise jeans I've tried on: Uncomfortable and a complete hassle. Let's just say I was ready to get home and ready to put on those pajamas..

Loves that set the bar too high

Many young women fall in love as teenagers, aspire to marry their high school sweethearts, stay in the little small town which they were raised in and have babies. Being the best housewife one can be is a normal goal. However, other women seem to be born with dreamer blood and cannot shake the desire to run free. These women are determined to cut the apron strings at a young age. They dream of exploring the world and being independent, before ever truly worrying about finding love.

Oddly, I apparently fell somewhere in between the two. As a little girl, I did always dream of finding love, but more than anything, I think I dreamed of having the best of both worlds. I very strongly had the desire of love *and* career. Then I went through a phase (the phase I'm still getting out of) when I decided love would slow down my goals and impede my progress, so I made it "wait," or only fell for unavailable men who weren't ready for serious commitment with anyone…because deep down, I wasn't ready either. However, as I've stated before: Deep down, I am a huge sap. Yep, a hardcore, hearts and flowers, slow kisses and candlelight, sap.

Maybe it's the fact that I grew up around such a magical story: The love story between my parents. Sometimes I think their storybook courtship really just set the bar too high. Some little girls dream about finding their guy on the beach, at college, on a luxurious cruise, at the club, or some social event…but me? I always dreamed of my parent's story. I used to ask Mom to retell it to me again and again, and I would look through old albums and read their old cards and letters in amazement. Everything from them meeting on the farm, to mom pinning a note on dad's tree, to dates at the old Dairy Queen - it all sounded like a dream come true to me and the kind of story that would give Holly Golightly and Paul Varjak a run for their money.

Just as I found myself having misconceptions about the Disney princess love stories, I also found myself thinking I would have the same love story as my parents. As a six or seven year old girl, I just happened to believe that Mr. Right would show up at our family farm when I was about nineteen, and that he would sweep me up off my feet, and we would ride off into the sunset and live happily ever. Nope. Didn't happen. Not even close. In fact, I have decided that if strike-outs were instead grand slams, fumbles were touchdowns, and air balls were nothing but nets, I'd be in the dating hall of fame by now. I'm pretty sure I am however in the hall of shame, regardless.

I guess as a little girl I didn't anticipate the breakups, the liars, the cheaters and the smooth-talkers. What little girl does? The older I got, the more picked over I started finding the selection to be. I simply wasn't willing to scrape the bottom of the barrel, and soon had to come to the realization that I wouldn't get a love story exactly like my parents. That was a little disappointing to me. Okay, maybe a lot disappointing. Perhaps, crushing.

Alright, single readers. I know you can relate. We all know of these stories that are so cute they seem like the perfect fantasy. When we watch a happy-in-love couple who has been married 35 years, I think it can definitely give us hope. However, we can become so wrapped up in the silver screen, a storybook romance, or a model relationship in front of us that we may fail to see something great which is labeled slightly different. However, who can blame us when these amazing stories have set the bar so high?

Time is flying, but routine remains

Have you ever noticed in the midst of your reoccurring heartbreaks, time appears to be flying? I have, folks. I swear it seems like it speeds up as soon as you enter the lovely dating world - almost as if time is just dying to run your hourglass out of sand just to turn you into an old maid! Page after page, chapter after chapter, everything is the same… just a little different. You know - you occasionally add some new names and new problems to the equation in replacement of any old names or old problems you may finally decide to drop along the way, but at the core…things remain the same ole': Still single, more confused than ever, and jaded beyond belief. The time/routine struggle goes something like this:

"It feels like Christmas was three months ago, yet it's suddenly three weeks away again?"

"I told myself I'd be bringing someone home for Thanksgiving this year. Well, I've been saying that for YEARS…but ya know, there is ALWAYS next year."

"Is it REALLY time for another birthday? THIS birthday is going to be the one that sends me into a crisis."

"The dating book which I read as a teenager now has yellowed pages!?"

"How are my best friend's kids ages 12, 9, and 5 when I haven't even started yet?"

"Have I really been at that job for that many years already?"

Is it starting to get to you? If you're normal, it likely is…just a bit. If not, please, please write us a book about how to NOT let it get to the rest of us.

Is this really my life? I dreamed of something much different.

Okay, so this kind of goes with the last two universal struggles. I may actually get serious here for a bit. Is that acceptable here? Either way, I'm going to shift gears.

I think it's obvious that almost all of us grow up dreaming of our wedding day, whether we want to admit it or not. Some likely dream about it more than others though. I think the funniest aspect of our early daydreaming is how wrong we end up being when it comes to what we wanted then and what we want later. The contrast is usually severe.

I had one of my epiphanies on this matter while having dinner with my brother and cousin at a fairly upscale restaurant (yeah, it MAY be good enough for the movies). But anyways, in between our conversation over brown buttered spaghetti, we noticed a table of high school students in their prom attire. When I looked at them, I didn't know whether I should feel nostalgic or sorry for them. Seriously…and I don't mean that in a bad way. They all undoubtedly looked sharp and had a fun night ahead of them, but having been their age a decade or more ago, I began feeling like I had secret insight which they didn't yet have…called "personal experience." In that moment, I realized I probably knew slightly more than they did about how things will pan out…yet I didn't personally know a single one of them. Now, of course no human being knows everything, but I'd say it is highly likely that their spouses and careers are going to be different than what they were planning on at that very moment.

As I looked at that table of approximately ten gleaming high schoolers, I thought about the fact that this night would always be a memory for them. I was witnessing a memory in the making which they will always carry with them. That moment would be something which would live on in their hearts no matter who they marry, or where their futures take them. I told my eating buddies that realistically, one of those couples at that table may last and make it to the altar, but probably most of them have a bunch of upcoming relationships they innocently know nothing about just yet. I didn't stop there though. I expressed that life will likely take them all down much different paths than what they are planning career-wise and maybe even location-wise.

Interestingly I even thought about a common result I've seen happen in my own small town: Unlikely couples always happen a decade later. Maybe Missy and Mark never dated or had any interest in dating one another during their high school days. They had nothing in common, and one seemed to be in a different league than the other. However, later on down the long road of life, the timing is right, and they surprisingly marry. Likewise, I pointed out that one of those girls at that table may still marry one of the guys at that table, but it may not be the one she's sitting across from. It may be her friend's current boyfriend who is sitting four seats down from her instead. I knew right then and there too, that one of those friendships may even sadly break up. Someone else sitting there is likely going to marry someone who no one expects, and will possibly go into a career which doesn't seem anything like who they are right now.

I knew right then and there that a lot of life was and is yet to be lived for all of them. I almost felt like I was Uncle Scrooge taking a glance back at my past or a physic (I don't believe in them) trying to predict the future, but that moment held a lot of truth. I was reminded that our first loves are seldom our lasts, and there is so much which is unforeseen throughout all steps of life.

It also caused me to drift back to my first love and my high school dances. I remember every single prom to this day. Prom was undoubtedly a special night, and quite honestly, sometimes I wish I could feel that much excitement about simple things like that again. I felt so free, so alive, and like the entire world was in my hands. My hair was carefully pinned up with about 800 bobby pins. I had the perfect do, the perfect dress, the perfect date, and even the perfect car to be transported in. I can still remember riding around in the convertible with the top down. I felt like we were celebrities on the red carpet and I can still hear and feel all the music we danced to. It is a night that will forever be a part of me, though the guy I shared it with was not meant to be my forever. I thought I knew it all back then, but I was so wrong. I just had no idea how the cards would end up playing out. The saying "If you wanna hear God laugh…tell him your plans," couldn't be more true.

So while I'm at it, I have a special message for any high schoolers who may currently be dating, struggling with relationships, or just plain living it up single and free.

Dear High School Girls,

Cherish every single moment of the ride. I know the journey isn't always easy and the days often pass slowly during this season of life, but rest assured, time will speed up the second you graduate. I once didn't believe the older folk who told me the same thing, but they were right. Now I'm passing along the message to you.

Decide you are determined to remember high school as a time of faith, purpose, fun, friends, family, activities, academics and a time to make as priceless of memories as possible. Take too many pictures. Get to know the cool (but respectable) tunes on the radio. You'll want to drift back later on and there's nothing like that feeling of doing so when you've grown older. Those songs will always keep you young at heart. Have fun with the latest styles (so long as you aren't letting it all hang out), but also be a trend-setter. No one is remembered for their "sameness" or cookie-cutter ways.

I encourage you to cherish your friends, your homecoming dances, your proms, the ball games, the clubs, the volunteerism, the activities, your classes, your teachers, your lunches, and of course your study halls.

Be a leader…not a follower. Realize your differences are precisely what will set you apart in life. Be a role model even when it's tempting to join the unruly crowd. Never become wrapped up in popularity. Invite your friends to church. Be the person who everyone wants to give the senior superlative of "Best Personality" to. You couldn't ask to be awarded anything better.

If you don't have a boyfriend – good for you - enjoy your singleness. This is your time to shine. Don't believe anyone who tells you that you need to be in a relationship while in high school. Hang up those posters of your famous crushes. Don't be in a relationship just because everyone else is. Enjoy everything else you have going for you. Start thinking about your goals and your future, but don't think TOO hard just yet.

If you DO have a boyfriend – good for you too. Enjoy your relationship, but don't put the cart before the horse. Great memories will remain from healthy high school relationships…even those which aren't made to last forever. Savor laughter and every moment from your goofy escapades with him. Enjoy the feel of his varsity coat when there's that crisp fall chill in the air. Have a blast cheering for him if he's an athlete, and support him in whatever activities he's in. If he's a good man, he will do the same for you. Treat him well, and make sure he treats you well in return. If he doesn't…let him go. The man God has for you will treat you with respect. Always cherish the innocence of first kisses – you will miss that feeling later.

High school is too short to be anything but happy. Make good decisions, and know that what may not feel like a big decision at the time could in fact change your life forever. I encourage you to hang on to your innocence. If you haven't done so though, just know it's never too late to rededicate yourself to a fresh start. The good Lord is all about second chances, and he's in the business of healing.

If you're in the midst of heartbreak, I promise you there's an excellent chance ten years from now (probably much sooner), that you won't even entertain the thought of the boy you're hurting over right now. If you're crying over a breakup, realize "this too shall pass." While our first loves always hold a special place in our hearts, just know that time changes so much, and anything that is truly mutual love and truly God's will, will make its way back to you – whether it's next week, months from now, or even years from now. There is so much ahead that you can't see. As hard as it is to believe, that breakup may wind up being the best thing that has ever happened to you (I know, I know)…but just wait and see, girl. This is so far from the end.

Don't hang on to anyone who brings you drama, and by all means, please don't start it. Life is a vapor, but it should be lived fully. Enjoy yourself every single day. Cherish your good friends. Dream of the future and work towards it if you can. Get your first job…it will give you experience and bring you a great sense of accomplishment, but don't forget to be a teenager too. Be that well-rounded person who your peers admire. Laugh it up whenever possible and always live purposefully for Christ.

Sincerely,

I was you

Finances of the single

Wow, okay. That last section got a little deep. Within every positive pessimist there lies a bit of hidden depth. Speaking of depth…many of us singles are in depressingly deep debt. (Try saying that entire sentence ten times fast). Don't you love how taxed to death we are? I mean everyone thinks we're SO rich. If we don't have a spouse or kids, we must have money to burn, right? WRONG! Most of us are broke… flat broke.. Helloooooo Ramen Noodles, plasma giving, thrift stores, and second and third jobs.

DECODING THE MALE SPECIES (THIS IS NOT A TRUE "HOW-TO" BOOK, REMEMBER?)

Ever wonder why some men will commit to one woman but not to another? Me too girls, but there are plenty of books out there on that sort of thing...this book is NOT one of them, in case you have forgotten that. However, I'm not sure I buy into those "how-to" dating books. I instead think about other possibilities:

"Does she have a mind-altering power over him?"

"Is he a fly on your wall, and he's seen you do something repulsive? Whereas, she somehow has it all together?"

Okay, okay..."Is she reading an amazing "how-to" book?" (I know, I know...I'm contradicting myself here, because I just said I'm not sure I buy into any of that, but MAYBE she found the ONE accurate "how-to" book on the market)?

If you've found yourself overwhelmed with endless confusion and winning at a losing game like I have, sometimes you need to step back and learn how to read men. Yes, that's right! Now, I'm not suggesting you play 20 questions with him, watch him like a hawk or chase him down like a desperately enraged, starving, out-for-blood, cheetah seeking immediate answers, but I am suggesting you privately design your own course of *Dating Awareness*.

Now, let me quickly say…I will never have all the answers, nor will you, but there are some very basic universal facts which apply. There are common terms and statements guys make and nine times out of ten, they mean the same thing. It's just some basic simple knowledge I learned. It's not rocket science, and I'm not extensively teaching you "how-to" read men, but I am pointing out some very common lines which come out of their sugarcoated mouths. These are some valuable lessons I have learned in the single's waiting room and from friends of mine. The truth is, what men actually mean often isn't what they actually say. Therefore, it's good to read between the lines and decode what they actually mean, as so often they certainly are not going to tell you what they actually mean. It could be they don't want to hurt your feelings, but the truth more often than not is: When a man fails to give the "true" cut and dry, black and white reason for a breakup, the female will continue to hold onto a false hope. Here are some examples of what I mean:

1. **He says**: I'm not ready for a relationship yet.

    → **She hears**: I just need to give him a little time, but he does want me. I'll just keep talking to him, seeing him, and putting my best into this. He'll commit to me sooner or later.

    → **Typically the correct translation for**: I don't want a relationship with YOU!

Now ladies, I know how hard this is for you to hear… especially if you're presently in this situation. It could be he really does want a relationship with YOU, but he is scared or holding back because he either just got out of a relationship, he's been hurt, or other various possibilities. However, a majority of the time this statement is usually his nice way of letting you down. Don't believe me?

Well, I asked a guy friend if this were the case after he recently cut ties with a girl he was no longer interested in. He told me he simply told her he wasn't ready for a relationship.

I asked, "You'd be ready for a relationship with your dream girl right now, but you just plain don't want one with her, and saying this is your way of trying to be nice. Am I right?"

He replied with "correct," and went on to say he simply didn't want to hurt her feelings, and he thought this would be the nicest statement he could make, and the easiest let-down he could give her.

Ever wonder why a guy has made this statement to you or a friend of yours, and then in no time flat he's got a new girl whom he's fully committed to (yet he wouldn't commit to you much less give you a real chance)? Maybe even a step farther, this very same guy who told you he wasn't ready for a relationship is engaged within a few months. It is in that moment when the dumped woman is blindsided by how fast he moved on. She then resents him for not giving her a fair chance and pegs him as a jerk. She feels lied to (well, she was technically).

Sadly, in the male mind, they think they are protecting a woman's heart by saying they're not ready for a relationship, but in reality, they hurt that woman worse because she keeps hanging on. His words give a ray of hope for the future. It would always be, I repeat ALWAYS be better in the long run if the guy would just gently admit he's not feeling it straight-up. The problem? Most guys won't. They just may in fact give you almost every reason, except the *real* one. This is why you must decode his words the best you can, ladies.

2. **He says:** I'll call you.

 → **She hears**: He'll call me.
 → **Typically correct translation**: I may or may not call you (it all depends on the man and what he's thinking when he walks away from the date).

3. **He says:** We're 85% right.

 → **She hears:** If we improve by 15%, we will be there, and we can make this work.
 → **Typically correction translation:** The 15% wrong outweighs the 85% right. You're not the one for me.

4. **He says:** "I just don't think you're the one."

 → **She hears:** Maybe I CAN be the one.
 → **Typically correct translation:** I just don't think you're the one. Something is "off," and I don't think we will ever be able to fix it. No amount of talking, begging, changing, or trying is going to make you my "right one."

5. **He says:** "I love you, but I'm not in love with you."

 → **She hears:** *Confusion*
 → **Typically correct translation:** Something is "off," and I don't think we will ever fix it. I love you as a friend and hope life treats you well, but you don't make me weak in the knees.

The "You're so amazing, but I can't be with you," line

Today, many girls are hearing a common line right after they get their hearts ripped out, and it goes something like this:

"You're one of the most amazing people I've ever met! You're gonna make some guy so happy someday..If I ever meet him, I'm gonna tell him how lucky he is!"

Yeahhhhhhh…Okay!? Have you heard this very disturbing line? What a doubly loaded bullet of flatter-schmatter packed with let-down insult to injury all in one. Like seriously..if he's so envious of this other guy's prize, then WHY THE HECK did he not snag her before the other lucky Joe Schmo came along!? After all, he had dibs on this beautifully amazing girl, FIRST! HE was the original lucky one…but he didn't want it? Hmmm…something doesn't add up, now does it? What does he really mean by quoting this line? I have no clue ladies. Your guess is as good as mine, but I can assure you that you're probably not his "one."

The "You're so amazing," line makes me think of ABC's "The Bachelor." If it's not enough to have your heart broken privately, these women sign up knowing they may get their hearts shattered on TV. I've noticed a common theme as the rose-less women are escorted away in the "ride of rejection."

Through tears, they almost always say, "I'm always told how amazing I am. I'm always told how good I am, but why doesn't anyone give me a chance? Why doesn't someone just show me how amazing I supposedly am? I'm ready to love someone, and I'm ready to be loved in return."

Now, I'm paraphrasing and mixing it up a bit, but so many of the women say dang well near the same thing upon getting their hearts broken. The "You're so amazing" line is clearly a common confusion in today's world. Are some women really too good, too smart, too strong, etc?…Or is there something "wrong" with her which causes him to run, and he just doesn't have the guts to tell her? Likely she's just choosing the wrong men, but in a woman's head, she's asking herself why she's not enough. Okay, it's a mystery, and I'll never be able to solve it…nor will anyone else. Moving right along…

The Busy Excuse

Have you ever noticed that every guy's favorite excuse for dropping off the face of the earth is "I've been busy?" Well, I've got news for you ladies. If you haven't heard from him in a real good while, he *has* been busy…*real busy*…but not in the way you think…at least nine times out of ten.

I know you're telling yourself his new job takes up to fifteen hours a day, and when he's not overwhelmed with corporate e-mails, he is spending his other nine hours with his intramural football league. Then there's his volunteerism with little kids, and not to mention, his activities with his friends at assisted living. He simply doesn't have even 30 seconds a day to send you a text and let you know he's thinking of you.

Want the hardcore truth(s) (at least much of the time)?

1. He simply isn't appreciating you enough to make time for you. Every guy can spare a little time for the girl he wants.
2. He just might be busy with that little busty brunette who has been posting all over his Facebook wall. That is what his volunteerism and activities have likely been consisting of, okay? He has been "volunteering to assist her with her needs," and you probably don't want to know any more than that. Anytime you've been dating the wrong kind of guy from the beginning, and he stops needing your attention, he's likely getting it somewhere else. "I've been busy" is usually a translation for…"I've been busy with another girl." Take the hint and run, sister. I know you're working to change the world, and all she's working is that new pushup bra, so therein, lies my point; If he wants the girl who has nothing to offer the world but some cleavage, he simply isn't worth *your* valuable time.

Back to "I haven't heard from him!!"

Don't you love that moment when you think for a split-second that the beep of your phone could be your new love interest texting you? Yes, we all do…but it's probably your mama texting to find out if you're home yet. Yes, you love hearing from your favorite lady, but you really got excited that you might have run across a man who actually makes a little bit of sense. Honey…put that cart back behind the horse, before you get trampled with disappointment.

Yes, another harsh truth which reminds us we are not living in the movies is the dreaded and unfulfilled anticipation that occurs in waiting for the call or text that never comes. We discussed this earlier…I know, I know, but it just has so many layers to it.

So you went out on a date with him, had a great time, and as far as you were concerned, you two were a match made in Heaven. Like socks and shoes, salt and pepper, a pen and paper, it seemed reasonable to believe the two of you shared an amazing connection! Right? Well, I mean why hasn't he called yet?

"Was it something you said?"

"Is there another girl?"

"Has he lost interest?"

"Did he think you didn't like him?"

"Seriously, what could keep this priceless catch you retrieved in the river of love from calling you back!?"

"Did he lose your number?"

"Did his 96-year-old great-great Aunt Edna pass away?"

"Did he break his hand, and he's unable to dial your number?"

"Should you call him?"

Absolutely not, sister! Stop freaking out, and tuck your crazy back in. Chances are…dude is just fine. Dude is probably better than fine. There are several possibilities as to what may be going on in this case:

Perhaps, he is playing hard to get or wants to see how aggressive you are…

Maybe it's the dreaded three-day-rule…

Or maybe he didn't feel the same connection you did. It's a harsh reality but a common occurrence...

Sometimes we just have to wait and see. Sometimes we just have to accept that our daydreaming of our wedding day with this new-found person may in fact be one-sided. While we're daydreaming about the location, the reception, the invitations, the flowers, the elaborate décor and our guest list (which includes the governor)...it's sadly quite possible that our wanna-be-groom-of-choice is kicking back with a beer and a video game, or perhaps talking to his roommate about the hot new chick at work.

Now, it could be possible he has a breakup to overcome, that he's going through life trials, or you have to "grow on" him before he realizes what you mean to him, and yes, maybe you will get that dream wedding with *that guy* someday..but don't sell yourself on those ideas.

Instead, live your life as though he hasn't slowed you down on your quest of finding love. Continue to do what you love and remember that long hours of excessive obsessing, waiting for your phone to ring, and loss of sleep gets you nowhere. Easier said than done, right? I know girl. I hate the reality of it all just as much as you do...but sometimes we have to face it...and keep on keeping on.

And don't...I repeat don't...torment yourself with constantly checking up on him either on the internet or through mutual friends. Chances are his Facebook page hasn't changed from the last time you looked at it thirty seconds ago...but then again, when you're on it 24/7...its bound to change at some point. In all seriousness though, my friend...don't torment yourself with this form of emotional insanity.

Lack of compatibility:

Though I still know next to nothing about the male mind, I absorb any hints my male friends give me about their strange species. Interestingly, I have learned lack of compatibility seems to be a huge issue. Remember my blue jeans scenario? Well, that's how many of them think. A girl can look exactly how a guy wants, but if something doesn't click, he's most likely going to be "out" eventually.

My friend Steven explained his continual unwillingness to commit to a certain girl by saying this, "My version of camping is in a tent in the wilderness, having to cook your own food and do your business outside, while being aware of bears and other critters. Her version of camping is in a Winnebago in Central Park by the Plaza Hotel ordering caviar."

Needless to say, her high maintenance was and is a deal-breaker. He knows she's not the one, but he does enjoy having a fling with her about once a year…every year. It also didn't help that after one week of dating…she told him he was the one.

Steven also clued me in that any girl who has to live down the street from her parent's house probably isn't going to be the girl for him. Heck, anywhere is good with him. Just as long as he's on the same planet as his family, he's fine.

HOPE FOR THE POSITIVE PESSIMIST

Have we discussed the awesomeness of flying solo just yet? We haven't? Oh goody! There are seriously so many awesome perks of being single, you whiners! You can have the place as messy as you want, be as selfish as you want, and you don't even have to cook. While your friends are sweating over the stove (or getting third degree burns) as they lift that casserole from the oven that their kids won't eat anyways, you are burn-free and no one is complaining that you grabbed you some Chinese takeout yet again…Yes, that's right. You are the only mouth that you have to feed, and you don't have to cook to make yourself happy with yourself. While the enslaved moms out there are washing dishes and cleaning up for the rest of their evening, you've got your feet propped up on the coffee table watching reruns of "Grey's Anatomy." *Sigh*…that McDreamy is something else. As long as you can see him every night, you're good.

Oh, and since you don't have anyone in your life, you also don't need constant reassurance from anyone. Nope, you can be ridiculously pleased with yourself. You can stay up or out all night if you desire, you can take up the whole bed, and you can pretty much do whatever you dang well please.

Okay, I get it. There are the down-sides too, but aren't those what the book has been poking fun at the whole time? The positive pessimist just doesn't spend their lives dwelling on those cons, because they're way too busy laughing about them, and writing their novel. Plain and simple, they're just too positive..

So anyways, it's hard for me to be serious at times, but sometimes a girl needs to tone it down for a bit. Though I can make just about anything into a joke, there just isn't any humor in some scenarios. Like the high school girls section, I have to pull myself together occasionally. So here's the thing: I have learned a thing or two that I think could potentially help those who find themselves twiddling their thumbs in the single's waiting room. As much as I believe faith and laughter to be the ultimate answers in this dysfunctional dating world we are all living in, every positive pessimist who laughs in the face of adversity is probably going to have their days of wondering "why" their journey has been the way it has been. Not only will the days of "Why?" hit, the days of "Am I going to be alone forever?" will likely hit just as often. Unfortunately, there isn't any good black and white or cut and dry answer as to why some struggle with their relationship life more than others. Ultimately, in all seriousness we all just need to believe that everything happens in God's timing, not ours.

When something we so badly want doesn't work out, or we can't understand why we can't find that "one," we need to trust God is saving us from something and for something. Any woman or man who has been single a little longer than they planned to be shouldn't look at themselves as a failure, nor should they compare themselves to everyone their own age. They should honestly be excited, because apparently God is working out something really special for them. (I can see you maybe rolling your eyes right now, because you maybe hear this a lot, but hear me out). That is not to say that waiting doesn't hurt, because it does at times. However, if you're "waiting," God has a divine purpose for it. You just need to be willing to release your grip, and willing to let him orchestrate his plan for you. Just do yourself a favor and don't prolong your blessings by wandering in the wilderness and running back to that which you must release first. He wants to bring you something better than you can ever imagine, but your hands must be empty in order to receive it. If you have already laid everything at the foot of the cross, you have done the right thing. Just be still, know that he is God, and that he will be right on time.

Reroutes and unforeseen turns can bring the most exciting outcomes. There is a reason for every single person who is currently walking on the path less traveled. Nothing God plans is in vain. How we view our heartbreak, our disappointments, and our story is entirely up to us. I choose humor, and I choose hope. Yes, I'm a positive pessimist, which means I am critical of dating, but I haven't written off the possibility of being swept off my feet by a good man reserved specially for me either. To be a positively pessimistic dater means to exercise caution, to remember what you've learned, and to laugh it off if it all goes south. A positive pessimist knows what's in their rearview mirror – all the good and all the bad. I choose to laugh at it, and I choose to encourage others to do the same. As aforementioned, a positively pessimistic dater isn't pessimistic about life in general. They are full of positivity, and in my personal definition, they believe in the Lord's plan for their life… whether or not it includes a husband, children, and a white picket fence.

We all can trust in Psalm 37:4, "Take delight in the Lord, and he will give you the desires of your heart." Now, this verse is probably one of the most taken out of context verses out there, and it tends to stir up questioning within a Christian. I'm not a pastor, but over time God has really spoken to me about this particular verse and the true meaning of it. How can this apply to dating? I believe if you truly desire to have a spouse one day, God knows that, and as long as you are trusting in him, he will see to it that this desire comes to pass. It probably isn't going to happen early, but it definitely isn't going to happen late. He is the Lord of perfect timing. This scripture doesn't mean that he will orchestrate a marriage that isn't meant to be. Sometimes what we desire at the moment isn't what we will desire 20 years from now. God knows the past, present, and future. He knows if our desire is a good choice for our life or a poor one. If your "desired spouse" doesn't match up with his plan for your life, he cannot grant your request if you're truly trusting him. It usually hurts when a person comes to the realization that their current desire is not meant for them, but down the road, they won't even entertain the thought of their previous desire once God's plan has come to pass. Eventually you WILL want God's desire for you…his desire will be your desire if you're seeking him. He loves you too much to send you someone who will never excite you or match up with you. He can and will send you someone who you are not only spiritually connected with, but yes, someone who you are also physically attracted to. He loves you too much to give you anything less than everything you've dreamed of and more. Blessed are those who wait for his direction.

The key is to not beat yourself up over the past, nor to dwell on anything which is beyond your personal control. Past mistakes simply can't be changed, but apologies can be made. Sometimes things just are what they are, but those broken pieces can form your story. Stop looking in your rearview mirror, and begin enjoying the view from your windshield right now…even if it is a junkyard. By all means, enjoy that junkyard, laugh it up, jot down some memories, and realize there could be a prize under all that wreckage. If you keep laughing through all this chaos, you will one day realize you laughed yourself all the way to the altar – because positive thinking yields positive results. Envision yourself laughing with your girlfriends as you go shopping for your dream gown, but for now – treat yourself to a new classy little black dress, and then find somewhere to wear it.

Once again, I can't give you any special formulas. As far as I know there isn't any infomercial item out there called "Instant-Date," nor is there any true "male decoder product"…at least not that I've heard of. So many singles are in the same boat of confusion. However, we don't have to sit around and mope about our circumstances. Yes, we just spent many pages laughing at dating's negativities together, but as long as we don't let our disappointments rule our lives and keep it in laughter and learning mode, it is all in good fun. Here are my short and sweet tips for living happily as a solo lady:

1. Church and prayer. Despite all of the chaos in the world, we can have hope, we can find healing, the truest love, forgiveness, and purpose in the Lord's house…single, taken, or somewhere in between.

2. Again, learn to laugh at yourself and the crazy dating situations that happen to you. I don't know about you, but some of my crazy situations seem like a movie…just not a chick flick… at least not one with a "happily hitched" ending thus far. The first key to laughing off heartbreak is to realize that life is not a movie, nor will it ever be. Wouldn't perfection get boring? Do not get me wrong. I am the first person to pop in a movie in the midst of a real life heartbreak. While we all enjoy a good tearjerker and can have situations which resemble that of Hollywood, it is important not to dwell on our beloved chick flicks. The previous scenarios of Leah Gardowski seem all too common to real life. So many times our romantic bliss is interrupted by circumstances either brought on by ourselves or our partner. So many times our plans and our dreams of love are shattered by different directions, by dishonesty, or by someone else coming in to destroy our so-called fairy tale. Thus, we become victims of love triangles, cheating, disappointment and ultimately heartbreak.

3. We've heard it said that we shouldn't worry so much about finding the right person. That is some great advice, folks. Instead we should try to work on being the right person. Do you have the kind of qualities that you are looking for in someone else? Do you have a good attitude? Do you know how to laugh and how to have a good time? More importantly: What does your heart look like? What are your beliefs and what are your morals? Sometimes contrary to popular belief, men can be quite observant of who a woman is on the "inside."

4. Don't take advice from upteen friends. Yes, this is my third time mentioning it. Refer back to the earlier sections.

5. Have an outlet. Pour yourself into different interests, hobbies and activities. Do you enjoy painting? Does it relax you? Don't worry so much about making a living at it. Do it for fun, and do it for you. Are you a fitness fanatic? Keep pushing. Are you a singer? Sing your heart out. Are you a writer like me? Don't do it. Kidding. Writing is perhaps one of the best coping mechanisms out there. Keep a journal, write a poem, write a song…hey, write a book if you feel led. Are you currently bored with your life? Consider picking up some new hobbies. Give some new adventures a try.

6. Be confident in your appearance and secure in your own skin. If you're unhappy with your weight, develop a healthy plan to get your body to where you want it to be at the pace you feel comfortable with. Consult with your doctor or nutritionist if you're unsure of how to start and maintain. Whether you are striving for weight loss or not, simply walking or exercising 20 minutes a day is a huge stress reliever, and good for your overall health. Leslie Sansone's "Walk At Home" is a great standby, even on those days where you may not feel like "working out." Be sure to develop a consistent wellness routine. Also, why not try some fun new hair, some different makeup, or a fresh style? Set yourself apart, and allow yourself some pampering.

7. Meeting new people is also undoubtedly therapeutic.…don't think of it as "dating" if you're not ready for that just yet.

8. If you need counseling or life coaching…go do it. Healthy people recognize their need for a little guidance or extra support every now and then. Strive for overall emotional, physical and of course spiritual well-being.

9. Work with good causes – volunteer, etc. Give others what you need more of. If you need encouragement, give some to someone else.

10. Surround yourself with positive people. If you can relate when it comes to disastrous dating…share your stories and laugh like crazy together. Wouldn't it have been somewhat uneventful if

you always had yourself completely together? Don't become "anti-married friends"…but have a healthy balance of both single/happy friends and married/happy friends that way you can have variety and see both sides of the fence, and have the perspective of both.

The truth is, behind every positive pessimist there is a former love optimist who got their heart broke, and it changed their life for good. Don't live in the rearview mirror though. The past is called the past, because well, it's past. So here's the thing, friends: We shouldn't stop believing in happy endings (there, I said it), but why not be happy right here, right now?......Even if you are in the middle of nowhere without a map or a GPS? Remember that junk yard earlier? Ahhhh…there are treasures within it. You just have to be willing to look for them. Your junk just might in fact be gold one day. Your setbacks just might in fact be stepping stones.

So where am I at in this season of life as I end this book? How about our dear friend Leah Gardowski? Well, I think I can speak for both of us here, as we share the same overall positive outlook, where we remain cautious but also undeniably hopeful. We may not always know what's going on…in fact, we almost never do. However, we've lived to tell about it, learned from it, laughed at it, and will continue to do so. We are just enjoying the ride…every day. We look for new reasons to love the single life…not new reasons to dread it. It's a beautiful season of freedom and that's how we intend to treat it. Still, we hope to eventually find someone special to share our later chapters with.

Like Leah, I was taught that the dating world is one big game, and that I've got to be a participant to win, but a recent revelation is telling me otherwise. I don't believe lasting love is found in a game, or by following some checklist. Real love simply isn't a game, nor is it forced or manipulated. Real love happens naturally without strategy and without abandonment. Listen up ladies: Any man who only comes around during the time when you're rejecting him will never be the man to remain in your life long-term. He's there for the chase, and there for the game, but he won't be there when you give in. The right man will stick around and communicate his feelings. Even more importantly, actions will follow his words. So here's the deal: The dating world may be a game, but we can find love without being a participant in *their* game. That's right. Now, that's not to say that love doesn't take work – because it does. That's not to say you should become boring or lose your spark. However, my point is…if you want to suit up, go out on the court, and fight opponents for the same player…that's your choice. In that case you've chosen to enter the game, but ladies - maybe real love comes right on over to you while you're warming the bench, and asks you to go be a team of two. Maybe all the guessing and getting played is a result of getting ahead of God a little too fast, when all he wants us to do is wait on that bench with an approachable smile and a willing heart. Maybe real love doesn't require so much exhaustion, so much keeping score, and so much coaching from others. Maybe real love finds us when we're kicking back as a God-trusting bystander, and as a fan in the crowd of love. Maybe real love doesn't look anything like a chick flick, but unglamorous, imperfect love is the best kind in the end anyways…it's the kind that builds character and the kind that lasts.

When I do get my happy ending (yes, I said "when"), I no longer imagine applause from the bystanders, nor do I visualize a man chasing an airplane, or catching a yellow taxi to get to me. No, I no longer picture myself being chased down, caught, and then twirled around in front of a crowd of 300+ people. Heck, I don't even picture a big city view, or a fancy setting anymore, but what I do picture is finding something genuine and something real…something that will make every bad date I've ever had worth it, because in that moment, I will know that all along, I was being saved for him and he was being saved for me.

You know…In fact the winds of positive change just may be in the air as I write this. Is this where the sugar-free accounts end…or is this where they truly begin? To be continued?....

NOTE FROM HOLLY

Hello, friend!

First of all, I want to thank you for taking the time to read my debut book. I hope you enjoyed reading it as much I enjoyed writing it. Interaction with my readers is important to me and brings me a lot of joy. I've never met a stranger as I'm completely personable and reachable. With that said, I really hope to hear from you. I'd love to hear your stories and I'd love to hear your feedback.

There are ways to stay connected with me, and I hope you will consider me as an ongoing friend. You can add me on Facebook if you'd like, and I invite you to "like" my page www.facebook.com/ chickflickslie. I also have a Twitter which I like to keep fun and witty. My handle is @hollymarietong and I follow back. You can also visit my website at www.hollymarietong.weebly.com. Additionally, you can subscribe and stay up to date with my Pop Culture column http:// www.examiner.com/user-hollymarielyrics. I'm all about keeping everyone posted on the latest news in entertainment! Lastly, you can e-mail any feedback, questions, booking and or interview inquiries to hollymarielyrics@yahoo.com. I am currently available for various bookings, interviews and speaking engagements.

I also welcome and would appreciate your (hopefully good) review on Amazon. Simply leaving me an Amazon review will get you the chance to be entered into my upcoming special drawing, in which I will be giving away a prize. If you leave me a review, simply e-mail me at the above address, so I can get you entered and will know how to contact you if you win.

Again, thank you for going on this journey with me. I don't know what point you're at in life as you read this, but just know, you are loved and God truly does have an amazing plan for your life if you allow him to direct your steps. We are all in this together – single or taken. We all have a soft spot for love – and that is why this book exists. I truly believe if we keep the good Lord first…everything else will fall into place.

May you experience the joy of faith, love, and laughter every single day..

God Bless,
Holly Marie Tong

P.S. Now I encourage you to go read something else. How about (Jeremiah 29:11, Matthew 6:33, Exodus 14:14 & Proverbs 3:5-6)? ☺